PROMISES, THEN THE STORM
Notes on Memory, Protest,
and the Israel-Gaza War

MELANI McALISTER

PROLOGUE

In the fall of 2023, I was living in Cambridge, Massachusetts, as a fellow at Harvard's Radcliffe Institute. I had arrived with a proposal for a book project, but not for the book you are reading. Then came October 7. On that day, the long-standing conflict between Israel and Hamas shifted dramatically, as Hamas attacked Israeli towns and villages on the border with Gaza. Hamas fighters killed almost 1,200 Israelis and foreign nationals and took 240 hostages. Like many other people, I watched the news in horror, both because of the civilians dead in Israel and because I knew that Israel would likely launch a massive military retaliation. It did—and the response was far greater than almost anyone expected. Over the following weeks and then months, Israel's bombing and ground operations killed more than 35,000 Palestinians and injured 70,000 others.[1]

The journal entries in this book are from the fall and winter of 2023—notes written during the first several months of that war. They don't aim to present a full picture of the conflict, nor to speak for those who lived the violence of the war day-to-day. My goal is to tell the story of the early months of the war from my own distinct vantage point. I am an historian of US interests in the world, concerned with the role of culture and memory, with a particular focus on US relations with the Middle East. My political consciousness was shaped by the Reagan era and the social movements that arose in its wake. For part of the 1980s, I was a full-time political activist. From those decades until now, I have struggled with the reality and legacies of US power in the world: its global reach, its multiple wars, its economic might, and the environmental destruction it has caused. But I also remember and respect the multiple histories of people in the US, of all backgrounds, who have chosen repeatedly to fight for justice—for themselves and for others.

In the fall and winter of 2023, I watched with sadness and fury as the death toll in Palestine rose week after week, and political conversation in the United States descended into feverish acrimony. It was then that the personal journal that I have kept intermittently since my teens became something else: a site for processing and reflecting on the events that were unfolding so quickly.

The entries reflect on multiple moments in history but largely focus on two, bringing the 1980s and the 2020s into conversation. That conversation centers around changes in activism, the impacts of war, the role of poetry and music, and above all the relationship between cultural memories and visions of the future. The 1980s discussion recounts the story of Lebanese musician Marcel Khalife and the Palestinian poet Mahmoud Darwish, reflecting on their popularity as global icons of Palestinian resistance. That thread also describes some of my own experiences as a political activist in the 1980s, alongside the larger history of the Israeli-Palestinian conflict.

The second thread is a deliberately schematic account of the Israeli war on Gaza in conjunction with commentary on events that were happening in the US at the same time: particularly the remarkable surge in pro-Palestinian protests alongside the surprisingly broad recognition of the human impact of the war in Gaza; as well as the heated debates over campus activism, free speech, and definitions of antisemitism. This thread also highlights the work of several contemporary Palestinian poets and visual artists, whose work circulated in the US before and during the conflict. This art provided what John Berger described in another context as a "way of seeing"; it demanded that audiences recognize Palestinian suffering in the war by offering a compelling vision of Palestinians' full humanity.[2]

Thus *Promises, Then the Storm* tells the story of two wars: the armed conflict in the Middle East and the rhetorical and political battle in the United States. It is about Palestine and Israel, but also about the United States: about both the force of US power, and the moral and political divides within the US public.

The form of this book is admittedly strange—a journal that is political and personal, written as an outlet for my own need to process the first months of the war, but also in the hope of having readers one day. I believed from the beginning of this most recent round of conflict that I had a particular responsibility to respond. First, as an American—because of the role of the United States as Israel's most important and powerful backer. And second as a scholar—because I have spent much of my adult life thinking about the role of culture and media in shaping how people see their world, its borders, and the world beyond those borders.

I was writing to ground myself and perhaps others, but also to try and capture the rapid changes and confusions of the early months of the crisis. We live fragmented by both media and memory, but we don't know how to navigate this reality, nor how to speak in a single register about a world whose fractures are fracturing us. That has been the experience of many of us living outside the Middle East as we have tried to navigate the horrors of a war that is both far away and viscerally present.

As I write this, the war is ongoing. Soon there will be little of Gaza left to destroy. However this conflict ends, it is also a "forever war," whose violence and legacies will shape the Middle East, and the world, for decades to come. This book, however, is not only about war, but also about the possibilities for justice and equality—especially those that reside in the hopes carried by artists and advocates, against all odds, into the future.

If I have been serenading happiness
Somewhere beyond the eyelids of frightened eyes
That is because the storm
Promised me wine and new toasts
And rainbows

Mahmoud Darwish, "Promises of the Storm"

OCTOBER 5, 2023

In my office at Harvard's Radcliffe Institute, where I'm in residence for a year, I am working furiously on an academic paper about Marcel Khalife, a Lebanese musician, oud-player, composer, and singer. My desk is an unwieldy morass of marked-up scholarly articles and random post-it notes, but my argument is straightforward: Khalife mattered a great deal to some American audiences in the 1980s, when he used his singular musical voice to champion Palestinian rights and Palestinian lives.

Back then, Khalife wasn't broadly famous in the United States, but he was a beacon for Arab American audiences in particular. He played at high schools or small concert venues across the country, usually where Arab Americans were concentrated—in places like Dearborn, Dallas, and LA. The concerts were joyous and collaborative performances. People sang along in Arabic to songs they knew by heart thanks to pirated cassette copies of Khalife's albums, which had for years made their way across the Arab diaspora, handed off and recopied.

Khalife's songs in those years were almost all poems by Palestinians that had been set to music. One of his most beloved songs, "As I Walk," was written by Samih al-Qasim. There is a clip on YouTube of Khalife playing the song to a large crowd.[3] As Khalife performs, backed by a small band, the audience sings along. Partway through the song, Khalife stops both singing and playing, simply conducting the many thousands of audience members in their rendition of it. This music is theirs, their anthem, their language of possibility.

Khalife's concerts in the United States were spaces where identity was affirmed: as Arab or Middle Eastern, as immigrant—as *visible* in a country that either ignored your existence or vilified your people. The Iranian hostage crisis was a fresh memory when Khalife started touring the US in 1982. People from the Middle East and North Africa (Arabs and Iranians, but also Armenians, Kurds, Amazighs/Berbers, and others) had been labeled indiscriminately in the US media as oil sheiks, terrorists, or religious fanatics.[4] For his diasporic audiences, Khalife was a holder of memory and a respository of hope. His concerts provided a space where the act of speaking Arabic was not suspect, where the foods of childhood and the sounds of home were borne aloft on traditional instruments and Khalife's remarkable voice.

Khalife's fans also included a sprinkling of lefty solidarity activists. I know, because I was one of them. After college, I had spent a year in Cairo learning some unsteady Arabic. I had then landed back in the US with absolutely no plan for what was next. One day I saw an ad for a position as a political organizer for the Cambridge branch of a national peace group, Mobilization for Survival (Mobe). I was shocked and thrilled when I got the job. I packed my car and moved to Massachusetts.

At Mobe, the three staff members worked out of cramped offices in a church basement, but we had a vibrant membership and a lot to do in Reagan's America. Both in Cambridge and nationally, Mobe was one the few activist organizations on the left-liberal spectrum that included Israeli-Palestinian issues on its agenda. The rest of our work oriented around the major progressive concerns of the era: anti-nuclear weapons activism, the fight for sanctions on apartheid South Africa, opposition to US support for right-wing governments in Central America, feminism and lesbian and gay rights. We called ourselves a "peace group," which made sense because of the group's origins —'60s anti-Vietnam War activists who turned to anti-nuclear work in the 1980s. But the "peace" label was also another kind of indicator: we were too left-wing to be a human rights group and too moderate for the Marxist-influenced left. We stood in a cold corner of the 1980s progressive movement when we supported a two-state solution and negotiations with the Palestinian Liberation Organisation (PLO) as the representative of the Palestinian people. At the time, this position led the Anti-Defamation League to label Mobilization for Survival a hate group. I often sported a lapel pin with two crossed flags: one Israeli, one Palestinian.

That pin is an artifact of another era. It's been a long time since I wore anybody's flag. As I prepare the paper on Khalife now, I admit to myself that it feels pretty old-fashioned, my plan for talking about Palestine in a register of hope. Maybe that made sense 40 years ago, when Khalife was gathering crowds in joyful sing-alongs. But now? The Saudis are sitting down with the Israelis to make peace, and Amman and Tel Aviv are crafting a water deal.[5] How many people in the US are even thinking about the unfinished project of a Palestinian state?

OCTOBER 7

The news is hard to process.

Hamas, along with smaller groups such as Islamic Jihad, has launched a major attack on Israel, making a shocking breakthrough in the barriers and guard systems that divide the enclave of Gaza from the towns and settlements in Israel's south. The fighters—perhaps 2,000 or more of them—attack and kill a group of young concertgoers at a music festival, and then murder families in nearby towns. By the time it is over, over 1,100 Israelis and foreign nationals are killed; the majority are civilians.[6]

The details arrive slowly, but the facts are stunning. Hamas fighters (and others who joined their attack) managed to cut through the Israeli border fence at multiple locations, move past surveillance towers, security barriers, and guard posts, and make it into Gaza's border towns and kibbutzim. They killed randomly at the concert then killed entire families in the villages and towns nearby. There are rumors of atrocities. Hundreds of Hamas members were killed when the Israeli military finally arrived in force on the scenes of carnage. Some of the Palestinian fighters retreated, pulling 240 hostages with them into Gaza.

Much is confusing—there are contradictory stories, chaotic and evolving estimates of the dead—but two things are clear. First, that this is a massive security failure on the part of the Israeli government. And second, that civilians were targeted: young people listening to music, families in their homes, children and old people. It is said that this is the most deadly single attack on Jews since the Holocaust.

OCTOBER 8

I'm back in DC for the weekend, where my reading group meets. We're a cohort from across Washington, DC, although most of us teach at George Washington University, where I'm a professor of American Studies and International Affairs. The group started out as scholars interested in the Middle East, although the membership has expanded and reconfigured over its 15 years. It is my intellectual and political home, my most poignant friendship space in DC. Tonight, we talk about nothing but the attack. What was Hamas thinking? Why this? Why now?

Many of us have written about the Middle East in some way or another: one colleague is an expert on Palestinian refugees, another on Arabic literature; one has written a history of the Iran-Iraq war, another writes about international NGOs and humanitarianism in the region.

In the reading group, we all know enough about Hamas not to be surprised at the attack, but the news is still fragmented. It's difficult for us to imagine how or why they moved from the desultory exchange of rocket fire with Israel that had been the status quo in recent years to *this*—an attack so brutal, so coldly effective in its killing and in the depth of its infiltration, that it will surely bring down a massive Israeli retaliation on the population of Gaza.

Of course, we are deeply aware of the profound anger and despair among Palestinians that long predated the attack on Israel. Neighboring states had been normalizing relations with Israel: first Jordan, then the UAE, then possibly Saudi Arabia, all while violence rose and daily life deteriorated across Palestine.[7] By August of 2023, the UN had reported that 200 Palestinians had been killed by Israel's military or Israeli settlers in the first eight months of the year.[8] In the West Bank, settlements have ballooned to the point that the entire territory that is supposed to be the bulk of "Palestine" in some future state is checkerboarded with Israeli settlers, who continue to expand their control over land, sometimes forcibly taking farms and homes from Palestinians. The Israeli government has even built special highways that West Bank Palestinians cannot drive on.

And Gaza: under siege for 16 years, with Israel and Egypt both enforcing a blockade that limited everything (and everyone) that entered or left. It has become a cliché to say that Gaza is the world's largest open-air prison, but the reality on the ground is even more grinding and vicious than that: hunger, poverty, unemployment, low levels of health care, and years of stinking open sewers. (A new wastewater treatment system opened in 2018 but collapsed in 2021 because Israel was delaying or refusing approval for the electronics needed to keep it running.[9]) Gaza is not, however, a site of utter abjection. There are many beautiful places: the seaside is gorgeous, and there are blocks with lovely buildings and trees. It is a place of universities and schools, with a lively artistic community of poets and painters.[10] Still, the numbers tell at least part of the story: in 2000, about 10% of Gaza's population depended on food aid for survival; in 2017, it was 70%.[11]

In 2018, Gazans launched the "Great March of Return," in which protesters marched to the barriers that separate Gaza from Israel, demanding both an end to the blockade of Gaza and the "right of return" to their former towns and villages in Israel. The non-violent demonstrations were carried out every week for over a year. Israeli snipers were given orders to open fire on anyone who approached the fence. As a result, 223 Palestinians were killed and approximately 8,000 injured. Many of those were shot in the legs, now in wheelchairs or in constant pain.[12]

Perhaps Hamas hoped primarily to get hostages in order to negotiate release for Palestinians in Israeli prisons. Maybe they wanted to reclaim their status as leaders of Palestinian resistance. (Lately, Hamas had been mired in the quotidian requirements of trying to govern Gaza, while Gaza remains mired in the despair created by the blockade.) The name Hamas gave the operation, Al-Aqsa Flood, points to the struggle over control of holy sites in Jerusalem. One thing is for sure: if the goal was to rivet the world's attention on Palestine, they have succeeded.

What happens over time to people who are pushed to the margins? When they are treated as disposable? How are they shaped by the losses that can no longer be counted? Langston Hughes once looked around at Black America and mused on "what happens to a dream deferred." "Does it dry up / like a raisin in the sun?" he asked. "Does it stink like rotten meat?"

Maybe it just sags
like a heavy load.
Or does it explode?[13]

OCTOBER 9

I first began thinking about the Middle East when I was quite young: a Southern Baptist girl growing up in a small town in North Carolina in the 1970s. When I was about 13, a friend from church gave me a book about the "end times"—how Jesus would come again when a certain set of events lined up in Israel, which would then lead to a conflict with the Arab states or maybe the Soviet Union, and ultimately global war. At some point, all good Christians would be taken to heaven directly in an event called the Rapture. The rest of the world would descend into chaos, ruled by an Antichrist.

All of this seemed utterly invigorating to me: my "good girl" faith was now connected with international affairs—you *had* to pay attention to global politics to see when God would begin to move. I started reading the daily newspaper. I got my hands on Hal Lindsey's *The Late Great Planet Earth* (1970), which diagnosed every political development of the 1970s as a sign of the end times. At summer camp, we sang the hit song from a popular Christian movie about the Rapture: "I Wish We'd All Been Ready."

Being a bookish kid, I also took to the stacks. In junior high, I discovered Anne Frank's *The Diary of a Young Girl* (1947).

I was totally shocked; I had never heard of the Holocaust. I read whatever I could find in our tiny town library. I watched *Exodus* (1960), with its moving scenes of Israel as the site of safety and redemption for Jewish people. The reality of yellow stars and death camps struck me especially hard, I think, because I was a sensitive white girl growing up in a sea of anti-Blackness, with few resources for naming, much less analyzing, the race rules that defined my life.

I arrived at the University of North Carolina at Chapel Hill in 1980, and my evangelical faith did not last long past my first religion and philosophy classes. But my identification with Israel didn't waiver. I was involved with Amnesty International, so I knew there were problems. We got "action alerts" about Israel's seizures of land and demolition of Palestinian homes, the building of illegal settlements in the West Bank and Gaza, the arrests and abuse of detainees. But the country of Israel still seemed special to me; it appeared beautiful in pictures I'd seen, rich with history and promise.

OCTOBER 10

Israel began airstrikes in Gaza immediately after the attack, targeting Gaza city and the surrounding areas. Photos and video showed plumes of smoke arising from the city, a mosque completely collapsed. Yesterday, Israel declared a "complete siege": a blockade of water, fuel, and electricity to remain in effect until the Israeli hostages are released.

Tonight, I connected with another Fellow at Radcliffe. She is Lebanese, a political fighter, a doctor, and a historian of medicine. Late in the evening—I was in bed but far from sleep—she and I texted about our fears of a regional war, deploring the devaluation of Palestinian lives so apparent in Netanyahu's decision to bomb populated areas in Gaza.

It's already hard to remember, but half of the Israeli population has been on the streets in recent months trying to get Netanyahu to resign. Crowds of Jewish Israelis protested his efforts to remove legal oversight over executive power, to expand his hold over institutions. If the protestors had succeeded, maybe a more liberal government would have come to power: people somewhat less determined than Netanyahu to expand the settlements, grab more land, push the boundaries for "Eretz Israel" (the land of Israel or Greater Israel). Now, Israeli security systems have failed. The military is humiliated, and Netanyahu is as hated as ever. But he is invulnerable as long as the country is on war footing. My colleague minces no words: "The alignment could not have been better—having right-wing extremist delusional corrupt criminals in charge with the foolish backup of the West."

President Biden announces that the United States will stand united with Israel, including sending a surge of military assistance to Tel Aviv.[14]

OCTOBER 11

In Israel, there is shock and horror. Many people still don't know if their missing loved ones are dead, or alive but kidnapped. Hotels in Israel have been made into temporary homes for residents who cannot return to their communities: many of their homes have been burned and are uninhabitable. There have been many funerals, sometimes four or five a day.[15]

The Israeli government is having difficulty giving an exact account of the number of residents who died: many bodies are burned, and some of those killed are Palestinian fighters. There are at least nine agencies or government programs involved in trying to find and count the dead.[16] There are rumors of beheaded babies, unverified.[17] But other images are more clear:

the mother whose body was found draped over her child; the father who jumped out of a burning house with his daughter in his arms. In Israel, this is dominating the news: the deaths, the bodies of children, the hostages.[18]

In Israel and also in various cities in the US, posters have appeared showing photos of the hostages. The "Kidnapped from Israel" posters were designed by two Israelis living in New York, but they are soon downloaded by people all over the world. They look like the missing children posters put out by US police forces, or like the photos of the disappeared in Latin America. I hear that in New York the posters are everywhere.

OCTOBER 12

Yesterday, the sole power plant in Gaza ceased operations after it ran out of fuel. In northern Gaza, hundreds, possibly thousands, of Palestinians have been killed by Israeli bombardment. The news is filled (if you look in the right places) with images of Gazans trying to dig out from the rubble: they pull out belongings, injured family members, bodies. A few days ago, Israel bombed a market in the Jabalia refugee camp, killing at least 69 people. Imad Hamad, 19 years old, died in the strike. His father Ziyad told a reporter about what it was like to retrieve his son's body: "The bodies were burned. I was scared of looking. I didn't want to look. I was scared of looking at Imad's face. The bodies were scattered on the floor. I recognized my son only by his trousers. I wanted to bury him immediately, so I carried my son and got him out. I carried him."[19]

It has been almost a week and there are still no foreign journalists reporting from Gaza. Israel has disallowed entry. In desperation, Palestinians are writing articles and posting on Instagram at a remarkable rate, trying frantically to get the rest of the world to see what is happening: to put a face and a story to the numbers.

Before all of this, I had been trying to wean myself from social media. Now I find Instagram to be my home base. The account @HiddenPalestine is a compendium—sometimes a deluge—of news clips, interviews, and some great historical documents. Sometimes there is an interview with Edward Said or Noam Chomsky from the 1970s or 1980s, documenting just how long people have been speaking for Palestinian rights. Sometimes there are interview clips from the US-based commentators: the dauntless Noura Erakat, Khaled Beydoun, or Amjad Iraqi. Gazans such as @byplestia, @queenofpalestine, @wissamgaza are also posting: so many images of the faces of frightened children, exhausted doctors, injured or dead bodies— mothers and sons and cousins and friends. Some people express opinions or post slogans I don't agree with, but I don't need to. The evidence of death and injury is completely overwhelming.

OCTOBER 13

Despite the daily flood of news from Gaza, I am working hard to put together an account of Marcel Khalife's life and work in the 1980s, to understand what brought him to sing about Palestine as his central theme for so many years. The way Khalife tells the story, he was just sitting around his family home in Lebanon in 1976 when he found a book or two of Mahmoud Darwish's poems and really liked them. So he set some of them to music.

Perhaps it was that simple. Or perhaps Darwish's words sharpened and gave voice to Khalife's emerging pro-Palestinian politics. By the 1970s, Darwish was already the national poet of Palestine. He had been born in 1941 in a village that would be incorporated into Israel a few years later. During the 1948 war, his village was captured by Israeli forces and his family fled to Lebanon during what Palestinians call the Nakba (catastrophe). In 1948, about 700,000 Palestinians fled or were driven out and not allowed to return. A year later, however, Darwish's family snuck back over the border. Their home village had been destroyed, so they moved to a still-extant Arab village nearby.

Darwish then became a Palestinian resident of Israel, where he lived until he was almost 30. He was part of a unique generation of Palestinian intellectuals and artists who spoke fluent Hebrew and also had personal memories of life before the Nakba. He published his first book of poetry at 19, and his second, highly successful, collection in 1964, when he was 23.[20] That collection included what became his most famous poem, "Identity Card." It is more widely known by its first lines: "Write down / I am an Arab."

"Identity Card" responded to a particular political reality: Palestinian residents of Israel were second-class citizens whose villages and towns were under military rule until 1967. All Israeli identity cards noted whether the person was Arab or Jewish, and movement in and out of Arab villages was often monitored at checkpoints.[21] Darwish's poem began with a familiar, quotidian encounter—a Palestinian man facing an Israeli soldier at a checkpoint. "Write down / I am an Arab," the man says.

And my identity card number is fifty thousand
I have eight children
And the ninth is due after summer
Does this anger you? [22]

The poem goes on to describe the man's ordinary life: he works at a factory, his father and his grandfather are peasants tied to land which has now been taken from them. It ends with a warning:

I do not hate people
nor do I steal.
But if I become hungry

I will eat my robber's flesh.
Beware, then, Beware of my hunger
and my anger.

Soon after it was published, the poem became a kind of anthem among Palestinians, and across the Arab world: a staccato assertion of identity in a moment when Palestinian identity itself seemed to be either criminalized or invisible.

Darwish was writing in the vein of radical poetry— straightforward, less metaphorical—that was shaping poetic language and topics for writers across the world in the late 1950s and early 1960s, including the Beat poets and those in the Black Arts movement in the United States and younger poets in France, Germany, Chile, and elsewhere. Those changes in poetic style, and the call for poetry to be politically relevant, set the stage for what would soon become Darwish's global renown.[23]

After the 1967 Arab-Israeli war, when Israel occupied all of historic Palestine and beyond (the West Bank, Egypt's Sinai peninsula, Gaza, the Golan heights in Syria), a number of people on the US left began to become aware of the Palestinian cause. Several leftist and alternative magazines of this period reported sympathetically on what was still a very unsettled situation in the newly occupied territories. Some of those magazines (*The Great Speckled Bird, Liberation News Service*) also published translated versions of Darwish's "Identity Card" alongside their reports from the war's aftermath. In a few corners of the '60s US left, then, Darwish became a symbol: a Palestinian voice speaking to people who had, until then, thought very little about Palestine.

Sometime in 1971, Darwish went to Lebanon to join the PLO, which had moved its headquarters to Beirut after being kicked out of Jordan.

OCTOBER 14

Today, many thousands of people demonstrated around the world in support of Palestine.[24] These kinds of large-scale pro-Palestine marches are not unheard of in Europe, but there is something new going on in the US. I've suspected for a while that change was brewing; many of us who teach about the Middle East had noticed it in our students. For the last 10 or 15 years, there has been less attachment to Israel among Jewish students, and more interest in the Palestinian story among many non-Arab students. And with the US war in Iraq, there was also a slide away from the single-minded focus on Israel and Palestine. For a number of years, I had veterans from Afghanistan and Iraq in my classes, alongside student radicals who, after Iraq, talked easily about American imperialism. The fault lines were shifting.

The 2011 Arab Spring also complicated the conversation. We saw something—an uprising across several countries—that opened new avenues of both thought and feeling. I could talk, as I always had, about the many ways people in the Middle East and North Africa had struggled for democracy, but now my students could watch it unfold in the streets. There were indelible images: the chanting crowds in Cairo's Tahrir Square; marchers sprayed with firehoses; protesters posting on Facebook with images of the injuries they had sustained at the hands of police. People were putting their bodies on the line in non-violent protest in Tunisia, Egypt, Bahrain, and Syria. That commanded not only attention but great respect.[25] The rise of social media mattered too. It helped with organizing the protests in the region, but it was perhaps even more important in the US and Europe, where people had the chance to experience the democratic potential of getting urgent and unfiltered news from participants on the ground, beyond the official channels.

In the images from various pro-Palestinian demonstrations today, I notice how relatively young people are—in their twenties or thirties. They are also racially diverse: Black and Brown and Asian and white. This is new for any kind of pro-Palestinian activism in the US, but it makes sense to me. If they went to college, it was likely in the era after the Arab Spring. More immediately, the Trump presidency and Covid-19 wrought profound changes in our country. The people on the street today are people who can see *themselves* in the Palestinian struggle. They are a generation who have watched Black people be killed by police over and over, and then risked getting Covid to join the Black Lives Matter marches in the summer of 2020. Or they grew up watching Latinx migrants separated from their families at the US border—or have been separated from their own families. Or they were radicalized and traumatized by the destruction wrought by the Iraq and Afghanistan wars. They see the links, and it doesn't seem hard to understand. People in Gaza are being bombed in their homes. Children are dying *en masse*. Doctors are operating without anesthetic. Free Palestine.

OCTOBER 15

It is just over a week since the attack. More than 2,000 Palestinians have been killed so far, almost as many as died in the entire six-plus weeks of the Israeli assault on Gaza in 2014.

It's hard to get details. US-based journalists are trying to get information without access to Gaza. A couple of days ago, NPR managed get the head of radiology at Al Shifa hospital on the phone. Dr. Mohammad Mattar described the crowded wards, with people on the floor because the beds are full. "The smell of blood is everywhere," he says, his voice crackling on the phone connection. There are so many dead people that they have converted part of the ICU into a morgue.[26]

Two days ago, Israel, having already dropped 6,000 bombs on the area in the last five days, warned all northern Gaza's civilians to move to the southern half of the enclave: 1.6 million people have 48 hours to get to the south of what is already one of the most crowded places on earth.[27] Many thousands begin to make the trek. Those who are in hospitals (as patients or workers), those who are too old, those who don't have the strength to walk or the means to ride—they don't get out.

Perhaps some others are simply unwilling to leave their homes, remembering how Israel permanently confiscated the land of those who left during the 1948 war. (Some Israeli histories implicitly describe those who fled in 1948 as cowards or as fools who expected "to return victorious after Arab armies won"—as if fleeing during wartime was a moral failing, one that rightfully could cost you the only life you'd ever known.)[28]

In the southern part of Gaza, tent cities are everywhere. Khan Younis, a city of 400,000, receives almost one million refugees over just a few days. The United Nations Relief and Works Agency (UNRWA) announced yesterday that its shelters were no longer safe, with water running out. "For the fifth consecutive day, Gaza has had no electricity, pushing vital services, including health, water and sanitation to the brink of collapse, and worsening food insecurity."[29]

My partner Carl and I are in different cities most of this year, but our nightly phone conversations go long, as we unpack what is possibly going to happen. We both tend to think that we are unshockable, but every day leaves us at a loss. Carl studies military policy and war, and he is very clear that Gaza is so densely populated that Israel cannot help but know that any air campaign will inevitably kill massive numbers of non-combatants. The orders for Gaza's civilians to evacuate the north might look good on paper, but when the place they are supposed to travel to is collapsing from lack of space or services, the warning seems more like a fig leaf.

OCTOBER 16

This month marks the 26th anniversary of the second Lesbian and Gay March on Washington, held in 1987. I was at the march as part of the Mobe contingent: our group organized around feminist and Queer issues as well as foreign policy. The march was a defining political event of my life. The experience was so joyous, so full of self-confidence. It seemed to me as if the whole Queer nation was there at the March: the Radical Faeries wearing flowers in their hair, the "dikes on bikes," lesbian moms pushing babies, preppy gay men, just ordinary people of all races. We were two or three hundred thousand strong, and in those numbers, taking over the streets in DC, we felt so free.

And I say "we" because I identified fully with the movement. I saw myself as heterosexual, but I deeply felt the power and the life-affirming importance of the fight. We were in the middle of the AIDS epidemic, and people were exhausted and fearful from seeing so many young gay men dying. It was a time of mourning, and yet the Queer community had rallied to call for something expansive and transformative. During that long, joyous stroll around the white monumental buildings of official DC, we insisted not only that Silence=Death, as the AIDS activists put it so beautifully, but also that Queer=Power, that love is love, that there was a world beyond heterosexual norms that offered a distinctive vision of freedom. That was my first real taste of solidarity, of fighting for something not only because I supported others, but also because I wanted the world they wanted. My life too would be better if the world were more Queer.

The march also mattered to me as well because there were times when I had felt a little out of sync at Mobe. I was a decade or more younger than most of the core groups of activists. They were children of the '60s, older and more disillusioned than in those earlier days, but still ready to change the world. My political outlook had been forged in the Reagan years and my visions of the future were more pragmatic. I often gently joked that we really should change our name; wasn't "Small Changes for the Better" a more accurate description of what we could do? The Queer work, though, taught me something about fighting not just for change, but for liberation. It was about envisioning what had seemed impossible. It was world-breaking and world-making work.

The activism of the Middle East Task Force, on the other hand, was much more difficult. When I arrived in Cambridge in 1986, Mobe's Middle East group focused mostly on Israel-Palestine, although we also took stances on other issues in the region, such as the US manipulation of the Iran-Iraq war of 1980–88, or the US sale of military weapons to Saudi Arabia.

The activist core of the group was made up mostly of leftist Jews, with a few Arab Americans and some others. I came to love and respect those people deeply, especially because the rest of the anti-intervention and human rights world generally had no interest in adding Israel and Palestine to its agenda. The issues were "too complicated"; most people just did not know—and didn't care to know—even the basics.

Activists who had no problem supporting the ANC in South Africa or the FMLN in El Salvador were very wary of the PLO. The PLO was and is an umbrella for a number of different factions, but for many people in the US it was simply equated with terrorism. In the 1980s, it was not so long since the PLO's massacre of Israeli athletes at the Munich Olympics in 1972 or the spectacular hijacking of an Air France plane to Entebbe, Uganda, in 1976, which had been carried about by a PLO member group and Germany's Baader-Meinhof gang. In both cases, the Palestinian group's level of violence was not particularly different than that of guerilla groups in other parts of the world, but its targets and its timing were. These were attacks designed with a global audience in mind.

At the Munich Olympics, ABC Sports had turned into a makeshift news outfit, covering the hostage-taking events live on American television for more than 18 hours. Photos of the young Israeli athletes and their coaches were everywhere, as the world awaited their fate. In the end, all were killed along with most of the hijackers in a disastrous stand-off with German police at the Munich airport. The Entebbe hijacking, four years later, also dominated headlines for days; it ended with few deaths and a dramatic rescue by Israeli forces. These were spectacular and terrifying events. They were intended to raise the profile of the PLO, to get the attention of the world. And they did.[30]

The main body of the PLO soon recognized, however, that attacks on civilians were gaining global attention but turning world opinion against their cause. In 1974, Fatah, the dominant PLO faction, announced that it would no longer attack civilians outside of Israel, where it continued to consider "armed struggle" to be legitimate. In 1988, it went on to renounce armed struggle against Israel overall. Of course, there have been factions within the PLO that did not follow its lead, and other groups, such as the Abu Nidal Organization and Hamas, that operated directly in opposition to the PLO's increasingly moderate stance over the course of the late 1970s and 1980s.[31]

The nuances of Palestinian politics were generally far from the consciousness of most progressives, let alone Americans more broadly. Mobe's Middle East task force mostly tried to educate people in the basics of the Israel-Palestine conflict. We developed a slide presentation. We talked about US economic, political, and military support for Israel, along with the expansion of the Jewish Israeli settlements in the West Bank and Gaza. We sponsored speakers, such as the Israeli activist Uri Avnery, who helped found the Progressive List for Peace, an early alliance of Jewish and Arab Israeli leftists; and Raja Shehadeh, the Palestinian author who founded the

Palestinian rights organization Al-Haq. But they too were on the margins of political discourse, speaking about co-existence and Palestinian statehood when almost no one in the US or Israeli governments recognized any right to Palestinian self-determination at all. In 1979, Andrew Young had lost his job as the US ambassador to the UN for just talking to the PLO.

My dear friend Nancy worked on both Middle East and Queer work, and she taught me a lot about steadfastness. It wasn't because she was particularly hopeful about outcomes; she wasn't. But "winning" wasn't why she did the work: you try to be effective, to create change, absolutely, but you organize and protest because you *cannot* remain silent in the face of oppression. That's your victory: the refusal to acquiesce when the powerful are counting on your distraction, your sense of helplessness, and your exhaustion.

OCTOBER 17

The "doxxing" trucks that arrived at Harvard about a week ago are not going away. They drive around the streets near the campus, displaying large pictures of "Harvard's antisemites" on their sides, along with student email addresses and other information.[32] The trucks are sponsored by Accuracy in Media (AIM), a right-wing watchdog group that specializes in harassment of anybody who criticizes Israel. Its trucks and other "outing" activities are clearly designed to render its victims both humiliated and unsafe.

AIM's campaign here is focused on a group of Harvard students associated with the Palestine Solidarity Committee and Harvard Graduate Students for Palestine. Ten days ago, as soon as they learned about the Hamas attacks, leaders of those student groups released a letter on Instagram. It began: "We, the undersigned student organizations, hold the Israeli regime entirely responsible for all unfolding violence."[33] The letter went on to make an argument about the long history of Israel's occupation of Palestine and to describe the horrific conditions in Gaza. What the letter did not do was to directly condemn the Hamas attack on civilians.

This, in my view, was both morally wrong and a serious political mistake. What Hamas did was unjustified. Not even the violence that Israel had inflicted on Gaza and the rest of Palestine over previous decades can absolve the indiscriminate killing of civilians—the targeting of young people, the deliberate murder of children, the house-to-house hunt for victims.[34]

I do recognize, however, why some people on the US and European left will not criticize Hamas's actions explicitly, even if they bemoan "all loss of civilian life." Many people, myself included, see the Palestinian cause as a struggle of the oppressed, in which the overwhelming preponderance of power lies with Israel. In that case, there are those who argue that the focus should remain on the powerful. They point out, quite rightly, that violence has often been part of liberation struggles. Artist and activist Dread Scott made this argument in a recent essay, saying that we don't study slavery by making sure we first condemn Nat Turner's rebellion.[35] Nor do we any longer write Native American Indigenous history around the suffering of the white settlers, who were attacked in their beds, after all, and slaughtered—women and children included.

Still, whatever one thinks about the possible justifications for revolutionary violence—be it against slavery or apartheid, or for national liberation in Algeria—protecting civilians is one bulwark against the horrors of total war. I would also point out that targeting civilians is clearly against international law, but international law has been made a farce so often over the decades of this conflict that it often seems pointless to argue within its terms.[36] So I turn to something more basic: what I hope is a realistic sense of justice in a complex situation. I understand that there will be civilian casualties in war. But, even in the most asymmetrical fight, there must be genuine and serious effort to protect non-combatants. For me, anything else is morally and politically indefensible.

The Harvard students, however, did *not* celebrate the Hamas attack. Instead, they focused on the occupation and the ongoing violence faced by Palestinians as the primary dynamic. Then Accuracy in Media showed up on campus (well, just beyond the campus gates) with those trucks displaying the students' photos and contact info—an invitation to personal attacks, a threat. Many of those students are of Middle Eastern origin, vulnerable to the anti-Arab and Islamophobic sentiments that have coursed through US life for decades. Some of them are undocumented migrants from Latin America. All of them are caught in the middle of a witch hunt.

It is an inquisition that has been going on for a long time. Several groups have been organized over the previous decades specifically to troll American universities. Canary Mission, for example, uses publicly available information, social media posts, and anything else they can find to list "antisemitic" professors and students. There is no clear definition for exactly what speech might get one on the list, but it is clear that any serious criticism of Israel, or *any* indication of support for the Boycott, Divestment, and Sanctions movement, will land you there.[37] I made the list about ten years ago when I signed a petition by Jewish Voice for Peace that called on TIAA-CREF (the retirement fund for teachers) to divest from Caterpillar, maker of tractors and heavy machinery which was providing the equipment to bulldoze Palestinian houses. I find Canary Mission something of a joke. Their website is amateurish, and they make no attempts to make arguments, just insinuations and accusations. But then I'm not a young person looking for a job, or a junior professor hoping for tenure.

Many people I know have received far worse than their photo on a website: hate mail, threats, complaints to their deans, loss of jobs or postdocs. On Harvard's campus, we have learned that a dozen CEOs have signed a pledge, helmed by Harvard donor Bill Ackerman, not to hire any of the Harvard students who are members of any group that signed the initial letter. It is, of course, impossible for any CEO to know the membership lists of each of those groups, but threat nonetheless creates a climate of fear. Students have begun resigning leadership posts in their organizations.[38] At NYU, the law school is launching an "inquiry" into the conduct of the head of the Student Bar Association because of their commentary about the Hamas attack in a newsletter. The student has essentially been suspended from their leadership role. The law firm from which they had an offer has rescinded it.[39]

OCTOBER 18

Yesterday, the Egyptian talk show host and comedian Bassem Youssef appeared on Piers Morgan's *Uncensored* to discuss the war. A friend sends me the link with a big thumbs up, but I find the conversation painfully difficult to watch. There is a pretense of a civil conversation, but in fact the interview is filled with conflict and interruptions, the two principals talking over each other. Morgan, with his very British demeanor and determination to play the "reasonable" observer, tries to ask Youssef what a "proportionate response" to Hamas's attack would be. But Youssef is clearly furious at the very assumption behind the question. He tells Morgan he cannot say. Probably, he adds sarcastically, we should just kill all the Palestinians. Later, Youssef holds up a chart of how many Israelis versus how many Palestinians have died in the conflict in recent years. Every year shows many more Palestinians dead than Israelis, but, as Youssef points out, the amount of difference varies. "It's like crypto," he says, "the exchange rate is always changing." Morgan tries to interrupt but Youssef pushes forward: "My question here is what is the going rate today for human lives [...] for Palestinian lives? What is the exchange rate?"[40]

It is bitter humor but poignant, because since October 7 there has been exactly this question: how many Palestinians have to die in response to the killing of approximately 1,200 Israelis? When will the world community, and particularly the United States, insist that there will be no more weapons shipments, no more aid for Israel, until the attack on Gaza stops? Would 10,000 be enough to sicken the Biden administration? 20,000? What exactly is "too much" Palestinian death?

OCTOBER 19

My dear friend David calls on Whats-App. We met as undergraduates decades ago, both on the same scholarship program at UNC-Chapel Hill. He's a Brit, lives in London, works for a business school, reads lots of novels, and goes to a conservative synagogue. I go to visit him and his wife Julia and their three sons whenever I can manage to finagle my way to London.

When I'm there, I get to experience a bit of how David and his family inhabit their sense of Jewish values: the importance of discussion; taking on big issues about history, politics, and morality; listening to each other; intently engaging with the project of *tikkun olam*—repairing the world. In David's family I see how that sentiment is built from the ground—teaching kids to ask questions, to learn how to answer them, and remaining nimble enough to be able to change their minds.

On one visit about five years ago, we got into a discussion about free speech, and his sons were a little appalled at what I admit is my "free speech fundamentalism." They couldn't believe I think it should be legal to say awful things about Muslims, for example, or to deny the Holocaust. David, having gone to college in the US, is quite familiar with the American Civil Liberties Union's version of free speech, which posits the right to speech in almost every context. The boys were not used to this view, and they asked me how I could support allowing such vicious commentary.

I told them that, in part, it's because I myself believe some things that others consider beyond the pale. In the small North Carolina town where I grew up, for example, it seemed impossible to imagine, much less say aloud, that you do not believe in God. (I didn't learn until my forties that my own father was an atheist, and, even then, he insisted that I not tell anyone.) Another example: in Florida, there are laws now against teachers talking to elementary school children about gender diversity. I am appalled by this. I told the boys that I think that any but the most basic "Don't yell fire in a theater" limits on free speech are deeply dangerous for democracy. It might seem OK when the things *you* hate are being disallowed, but, in reality, anyone can suddenly find themselves among the silenced. We talked a long time. What was most striking to me, in the end, is how lively, respectful, and thoughtful the conversation was.

The visits go both ways, and David's family visit the US too. One son, now in his mid-twenties, was here just this past summer. While we were out on a long hike, he told me that Israel is his favorite country. He likes the way it seems young and vibrant. It matters that he thinks Jews are safe there.

David and I have always disagreed about the Israeli-Palestinian conflict, and we've been debating it together for 30 years. So, when he calls from London as I'm walking around Harvard Yard on this warm October evening, we jump right in. "It's terrible," he says, what is happening. I agree and we commune for a minute—before suddenly realizing that we are talking about different things. He means the attacks on Israelis; I am thinking of the number of Palestinian dead. Fundamentally, we both care about both, but we begin (and end) in different places. David agrees that the suffering of Palestinian civilians is awful. "But what was Israel supposed to do?" he asks me. "This was Israel's 9/11. They killed entire families."

I hear his anguish, even his fear. One of his sons easily might have been visiting there. They might have gone to the festival where killers descended on early-morning dancers. It feels personal and terrifying. And it is not, in fact, safe for Jews there.

David goes on to point out how close Gaza is to the heart of Israel. If Hamas is not destroyed, they could do this kind of thing again. I argue that the tight quarters work both ways. Israel has just rolled over the border, killing thousands, and giving a million more people just days to escape, if they can.

Besides, I say, if this is Israel's 9/11, do you think the US response is a good model? A two-front war that cost hundreds of thousands of lives, sowed the ground for ISIS, and left two countries devastated? All while saddling the US with a national debt that will shape the lives of our children's children? No, he says, of course I don't want that. But, again, Hamas is *so close*.

Later that night he texts me a map of the distance from Tel Aviv to Gaza city. As if it's the physical proximity, rather than the political divide, that is at the heart of things.

Yesterday, Jewish Voice for Peace and IfNotNow, two largely Jewish organizations, held protests on Capitol Hill against the Israeli bombardment of Gaza. Meanwhile, President Biden flew to Israel to hug Netanyahu.[41]

OCTOBER 20

Marcel Khalife's music in the 1980s was a case of political commitment in action. He chose support for Palestine when it was not easy—indeed dangerous—to do so. Khalife first came to fame during Lebanon's long civil war (1976–1990). That war pitted numerous political factions against each other, in multiple and changing alliances: Sunni v. Shi'a Muslims; Lebanese Christians, particularly the Maronites, forming their own militias; and the Palestinians often resented by almost everyone, their refugee camps generally considered a blight and a burden.

At the start of the war, Khalife had formed a small musical group (which eventually became the Al Mayadine Ensemble) and they began to perform in burnt-out buildings or abandoned lots around Beirut. When he released his first album in 1976, *Promises of the Storm,* four of the five songs were based on poems by Mahmoud Darwish. This very fact is remarkable. Khalife is a Maronite Christian, and of all the shifting coalitions that emerged in the Lebanese civil war over the next 15 years, one fact remained stable: the majority of the Maronites were deeply opposed to the Palestinian presence in Lebanon.

For Khalife to choose to focus on Palestine through Darwish's poetry was a remarkable choice to make in that place and time. He was not alone; there was a small group in Lebanon during the war who remained leftists and internationalists amidst factionalism, including Khalife's close friend the novelist Elias Khoury. This cohort deeply believed in the kind of pan-Arab solidarity that had come to be organized in part around support for Palestine. To do what they did—to stand as internationalist supporters of Palestine in opposition to one's own community in a time of civil war—demonstrates the kind of courage that builds bridges, that opens up connections where sectarianisms divide communities, that creates solidarity in the face of spiraling violence.

The title song of Khalife's first album, *Promises of the Storm* (1976 in Beirut; 1983 in Washington), was from a poem written by Darwish.[42] The song is both mournful and joyful as it evokes those who have been insufficiently loyal to the struggle. A storm may seem dangerous, but there is promise in the wake of it:

> Because the storm
> Swept away the voices of idiotic, obedient birds
> And swept away the counterfeit branches
> From the trunks of standing trees

The song first condemns those who say they support a cause but who cannot be counted on: the "obedient" and the "counterfeit." It then offers a promise and an affirmation, a sense that the struggle for Palestine is inevitably going to be successful:

> For from the time the storm began to rage in my country
> It has promised me wine and rainbows.[43]

This striking vision of the future looks to abundance and joy, even in the wake of the loss of all of Palestine in the 1967 war. An exceptional thing about Darwish and Khalife in those years was that they held onto a sense of hope in their work, even as the PLO was pushed out of Beirut to Tunis, and the Israeli settlements seemed to grow like desert mushrooms. They both gestured always toward a future Palestinian homeland, democratic and free. They sensed a future that is no longer easy for us to imagine.

OCTOBER 21

It's impossible to ignore the multiple ways that 2023 resonates with 1982. In 1982, a little over five years after Khalife's *Promises of the Storm* was released in Beirut, Israel invaded Lebanon in alliance with the Maronites, even as the Lebanese Civil War raged on. At that time, I was an intern at *Newsweek* magazine in New York. I had been assigned to be a fact-checker for stories about the invasion, which Israel said was designed to destroy the PLO's capacity to attack in northern Israel. I carefully double-checked the names of political leaders and the spelling of refugee camps and towns and as, day after day, Israeli tanks rolled across Lebanon shelling those camps and towns. On TV, smoke billowed from tall buildings, as the nightly news showed images of Beirut in flames. Israel quickly moved to cut off water and electricity to the city, a siege that lasted more than two months. The Palestinian writer Jean Said Makdisi described the eerie look and feel of a city being bombarded: "the sky orange with the unnatural light of exploding phosphorus bombs; the whizzing screams of jets darting for the kill."[44]

The idea, as one military official put it, was "to limit the [PLO] leadership's influence in order to provide us with greater freedom of action."[45] The Israelis also hoped to turn southern Lebanon into a buffer zone, and, ideally, to install a friendly, Maronite Christian government in Beirut. Despite these expansive goals, Israel's official military plan was for a 48-hour mission that would eradicate the PLO infrastructure within 40 km of the border before pulling back.[46]

Instead, the Israeli military pushed forward all the way to Beirut—90 km. Ariel Sharon, then the minister for defense, oversaw this expanded mission. Israel laid siege to Beirut throughout the summer, cutting off water, food, electricity, and transportation to the city of 600,000 for almost two months. In July, Red Cross officials warned that Israel's cutting off of electricity and fuel for generators put all of West Beirut's hospitals in danger of closing down.[47]

Palestinian refugee camps in Lebanon were targeted, with Israel methodically destroying Palestinian homes. One *New York Times* correspondent at the time commented that the destruction reminded him of Vietnam, when American forces had "destroyed a village in order to save it."[48] I wasn't old enough to really remember Vietnam, but I knew what I was seeing: people of all ages being killed and maimed by a powerful military simply because they were in the way.

The invasion of Lebanon changed something fundamental in my view of Israel. Without the sanctification of my earlier faith, it began to look much like every other country. Despite the media images of "brave little Israel" surrounded by "hostile Arab states," as the media pundits tended to put it, I just saw the asymmetrical unfolding of an army attacking a largely civilian population.

Three months after the invasion, Israel still controlled large parts of Lebanon. One September evening in 1982, Israeli Defense Minister Sharon allowed the Maronite militias into the Palestinian refugee camps of Sabra and Shatila that were under the guard of the IDF. Over the course of three days, the Phalange killed more than 2,000 civilians.[49] The Palestinians trapped in the camps were mowed down by the militias, while the Israeli military stood by—knowing, watching, silent. (Ariel Sharon lost his job as Minister of Defense after an Israeli investigation found that he was culpable for not using the IDF to stop the Sabra and Shatila massacre.)

Amy Kaplan has argued that the 1982 war was a turning point in US views of Israel overall, a moment when some observers, including journalists, stopped seeing Israel as inevitably righteous. NBC's John Chancellor commented at the time that what he was seeing in the Lebanon invasion was new: "We are now dealing with an imperial Israel, which is solving its problems in someone else's country, world opinion be damned."[50]

This "imperial Israel" was not the only perpetrator. That's the thing about Palestine: it has been occupied by Israel, but it has been failed by almost everyone. The Maronite militias and their allies were never held accountable for their murderous violence against Palestinian refugees. The Arab states have failed Palestinians time and time again, almost always expressing solidarity but rarely working for a real political solution. Powers outside the region have also been key. From its beginnings in the nineteenth century, Zionism had the (sometimes ambivalent) backing of the British. And since the 1967 war, at least, the US has been the fiscal sponsor and unstinting political backer of Israel's ongoing occupation. The world at large has watched Israel's steady land grab in the West Bank, its destruction of homes and violence against the civilian population, becoming animated once in a while only to return to a state of indecision or ignorance. Several scholars have pointed out that the "world community"—in the form of UN agencies and NGOs—has been well-meaning, but in practice has essentially made Palestinian dispossession functional, a matter of bureaucratic management.[51]

In addition to control over land and resources, there is another kind of power at work: the power of narrative, of memory. The invasion of 1982 was a break in the narrative of Israel as an "invincible victim"—Kaplan's term for the paradoxical image of a state and a people that was always in danger and yet impossible to defeat.[52] Events in Lebanon raised questions about both Israel's victimhood and its invincibility. Israel was clearly on the offensive in Lebanon, even in the view of mainstream US media. Even though Israel "won" that war, in that it forced the PLO out, it also bought itself another occupation. The IDF spent 18 years in southern Lebanon, departing only in May 2000. That occupation kept the PLO at bay, but it only fed the rise of other armed groups, such as Hezbollah.

Much of that is forgotten now. In the US, "Sabra and Shatila" means something only to Middle East scholars and some Arab Americans. That too is the violence of control over narrative. Hegemonic stories belong to the powerful, even in the face of significant evidence that counters their claims.[53] Chimamanda Ngozi Adichie's remarkable novel of the Nigeria-

Biafra war (1967–1970), *Half of a Yellow Sun* (2006), decries the public's ability to allow something as horrific as war and mass starvation to disappear from memory. Within the novel is another book, an account of the Biafra war written by one of the characters. Its evocative title is *The World Was Silent as We Died*.[54] Both books, Adichie's and her character's, ask how the world forgets what it once knew—jettisoning suffering, murderous rampage, and guilt into the dark corners of amnesia.

A year after the Israeli invasion, in 1983, the Iraqi painter Dia al-Azzawi made an extraordinary, haunting drawing in ballpoint pen and pencil. *Sabra and Shatila Massacre* is a monumental work measuring 9 x 24 feet: a claustrophobic montage of human and animal bodies, weapons, and domestic items. It is a defiant act of memory, depicting the scenes of horror and chaos that occurred in the refugee camps, rendered as a mass of figures and shapes sprawling across a canvas too large to ignore. For years it was homeless and almost unknown outside the Arab world. London's Tate Modern acquired it in 2014. It is delicate, however, so displayed only a few months each year.[55]

OCTOBER 22

Right now, the 1980s are like the underlayers of a palimpsest. I watch Gaza being bombed, and it seems like a turning point: different in intensity and horror from all that has come before, yet it is also reminiscent of the Israeli invasion of Lebanon in 1982. I look at young activists standing up for Palestine today and I remember my own years as an activist. Back then we didn't even use the word "Palestine"; instead we talked of the "Occupied Territories" or the West Bank and Gaza. We criticized Israel's occupation of those territories in 1967 but said little about the consequences of 1948. "I never thought I'd see the day," I keep saying to the people around me. So many students and just ordinary citizens are marching in support of Palestine. But I also never expected this kind of devastation either: Israel bombing hospitals, schools, libraries, and homes, leaving northern Gaza a wasteland.

How do memories converge and conflict with the current moment? Like many activists of my generation, I feel the weight of decades. What is happening today is part of that history, and yet also so different—resonant but not a repetition. These young people organize in ways that reflect the urgency of a war that is killing hundreds or thousands of people a day. In this way, too, I am reminded of Queer work and AIDS activism from the 1980s, when people were also fighting against an avalanche of death and suffering. They fought like it mattered desperately. That urgency directs me too. I was supposed to be spending this academic year writing a book about Middle Eastern and African literature and music in the late Cold War, and now I can only write about this war, these horrors.

I've picked up David Scott's *Conscripts of Modernity* (2004), a brilliant meditation on colonialism and postcolonialism that is also a primer on how to write and read history.[56] I've pulled it off the shelf because I need to think more about what it means for me to be writing these comments on the current war with the memory of the 1980s so vivid as a backdrop. On the face of it, Scott's book is a close reading of C. L. R. James's history of the Haitian revolution *The Black Jacobins*, written in 1938. But Scott also makes a larger argument about how history-writing (and I would add the writing of novels, music, poems, and journalism) encodes within it a set of hopes for the future. Scott focuses on how James's history of the Haitian revolution was shaped by his historical moment, his "space of experience." Scott wants to show that James's history-writing was also informed by his imagination of the future, his belief that certain things were still possible—a "horizon of possible futures."[57]

In the 1930s, when James was writing about Haiti's eighteenth-century revolt, the colonized world was overflowing with hope for freedom from imperial rule. As World War I neared its end, President Woodrow Wilson had famously called for the self-determination of peoples, a precept enshrined in the Treaty of Versailles that ended the war. The idea galvanized intellectuals from around the colonized world—many of them gathered in London or Paris or New York. In the 1920s and 1930s, there was something in the air at certain cafés where politicians and activists came together: future African presidents Aimé Césaire and Léopold Senghor talked in Paris, and George Padmore and Jomo Kenyatta sat together in London.[58]

In that pregnant moment, James wrote with an expectation of possible futures, a longing for a certain kind of world-to-come. His sense was that Haiti's independence in 1804 had launched the beginning of the end of empire; that soon, new and freer communities would replace the brutalities of colonialism. Today we know a different story: the frequent failures of formal independence to provide true freedom, and the ways in which postcolonial liberation was often far less liberating than its supporters had dreamed. The old order collapsed, but the new order was defined less by radical democracy and freedom than by the reach of transnational corporations, the hot wars of the Cold War, and local corruption and betrayal.

How then do we read James's anti-colonial story of a signal victory against colonialism today, with the knowledge that so many of the futures James and his cohort saw on the horizon were in fact stillborn or shattered? We must remember, Scott says, that people writing before us lived with "a horizon of possible futures that are not, any longer, ours to imagine, let alone seek after and inhabit."[59] Those futures have been foreclosed; we can and must find other possibilities, other narratives to shape the worlds we hope to make.

Scott doesn't say it quite this way, but I am beginning to think we should read the history and literature and music of previous eras not just as documents of the past, but as maps of imaginary futures (possible states, new self-definitions, hoped-for reworkings of social space) that once belonged to some people but perhaps are no longer available to us. We do still have options for imagining the world otherwise, but we cannot simply recycle the dreams of the past. In this sense, we read the texts of the past as reversible figures—both as statements of possibility in their moment and as grave markers for all those futures that never happened.

Marx famously discussed how revolutionaries often use the past to make their ideas seem thinkable, dressed up in "time-honored disguise and borrowed language" from previous generations.[60] The issue now, I think, is not that change can only be smuggled in under a mantle of tradition; the danger is that we will hold onto tradition when we desperately need change. We need to know when it is time to seek new horizons of possibility. I have long doubted that the decades-old horizon of a possible future for Palestine and Israel—the one that centered on two states for two peoples—can any longer be a useful framework in our present. Its demise has many causes, but fundamentally it was buried underneath the turned soil of the Israeli settlements that now dominate the West Bank.

OCTOBER 24

More than 700 Palestinians were killed in air raids overnight, the single deadliest day of the fighting so far. One of Gaza's last remaining medical facilities, the Indonesian Hospital, shut down. An Israeli army spokesperson says that Israel has attacked Hamas's "operational headquarters" and killed at least three deputy commanders.[61] Doctors

Without Borders posts a video on their YouTube page of a Palestinian doctor amputating a nine-year-old boy's foot. There aren't enough supplies to actually sedate him properly, and what there are must be shared among the massive influx of patients. The surgeons sit on the middle of the hospital floor, operating while the boy is under only light sedation. The boy's mother and 13-year-old sister are sitting nearby. There is no ambient sound in the video (only a voiceover), so we don't hear screams. Most horrifying of all, I think, is that the sister is watching, knowing that she will need surgery next.[62]

OCTOBER 25

The past lays over the present in such strange ways. We see earlier moments as resonance, as promise, as warning. It's not just the truism that people who forget the past are doomed to repeat it. It's that people search hard for a "useable past": something that offers hope or a weapon or a lesson. Being both an historian and, these days, practically an artifact myself, I sometimes cannot help but see how each historical moment takes its shape from what came before. But "what came before" is never just a given: we know it through our own or others' stories about it. And the future? It is, of course, shaped by our hopes and our behaviors: we just can't be sure which hopes or which behaviors will make a difference.

As a teaching tool a few years ago, I developed for my students the idea of "The Three Promises." That is, I teach the Israeli-Palestinian conflict in part by having us take up three historical moments when a promise was made to one or both parties. My teaching strategy asks students to set aside religious claims to the "Promised Land." The belief that God promised the land of Canaan to Abraham, Isaac, and their descendants has had an outsized impact on the history of the region, but it is not a promise that we can evaluate historically.

The three promises we analyze in class are modern ones, made and broken in the twentieth century by Britain, the US, and the international community.

First, the Balfour Declaration in 1917, in which the British promised a "Jewish national homeland" in Palestine. Second, the UN Partition Plan in 1947, which divided Palestine into two states, one for Arabs and one for Jews. And finally the Oslo Accords of 1993, which were supposed to lead to eventual statehood for Palestine. Of course, this is a gross over-simplification of the twisted history of Israel and Palestine, and I don't ignore the multiple other important moments when I teach, including the wars of 1948, 1956, 1967, 1973, 1982, and so on.

I want my students and I to think together about Palestinian and Israeli history in the terms that somebody like David Scott offers: let's ask what each party dreamed of in that moment, what hopes they drew upon to tell a national story.

In 1917, Lord Balfour, British Foreign Secretary, promised to a leader of the British Jewish community, Lionel de Rothschild, that the British would ultimately support a "national homeland for the Jewish people" in Palestine, which had been part of the Ottoman Empire. Jews had faced persecution across large swaths of Europe for centuries, and the still-young Zionist movement sought a national refuge. (Zionism, before the state of Israel was formed, was simply the movement to create a Jewish state.) When WWI ended, the victorious British and French carved up the Middle East into various "mandates," in which European powers occupied former Ottoman territories under the theory that the occupied peoples were being helped along until they were "ready" for self-rule.

For the world Zionist movement, Balfour's declaration was thrilling. The Zionist settlers who went to Palestine after WWI joined others who had arrived earlier. They were still small in number, and they were controlled by the British mandate just as the Palestinians who already lived there were controlled. Jews and Arabs lived and especially worked side-by-side, and they at times cooperated in areas such as labor activism.[63] The British, however, favored the Jews, supporting Jewish immigration and land purchases as part of its Balfour promise.

As Jewish immigration grew quickly in the 1920s and 1930s, Arab residents began to develop a distinct nationalist movement of their own, inspired by nationalist stirrings around the world, such as in Gandhi's India.[64] (This is also when C. L. R. James was writing *Black Jacobins*.) Palestinian Arabs launched a mass strike to protest against Zionist settlements in 1936, which led to the Great Revolt of 1936–39.

Zionism had been accelerating globally during those same years, energized by that same sense of national promise, if not necessarily its anti-imperial commitments. Indeed, at first, Zionists had tied their fate to one of those imperial powers, championing Britain's Balfour promise as binding on the world. As the attacks on Jews in Europe began to increase in the late 1930s, people fleeing Germany or Poland or Austria tried to immigrate to Palestine. Facing a potentially massive increase in immigrants in the middle of a contentious situation between Arabs and Jews already living in Palestine, Britain limited immigration—which is to say that it shut out Jews trying to escape the Holocaust. The Jewish community in Palestine responded with righteous fury. They now became *anti*-colonialists, with the more militant among them attacking British military and civilian targets—most infamously, a bombing at the King David Hotel in Jerusalem by the right-wing faction Irgun, in which 91 people were killed.

Looking back at this history, many scholars today, led by a generation of revisionist Israeli scholars in the 1980s and 1990s, describe Israel as a settler-colonial state. They are not wrong; the comparisons to the US and Australia, for example, are apt at multiple levels, including the continuing political, economic, and cultural dominance of the settlers over the rest of the population. But, as with both the US and Australia, Israel's story about itself is one in which it is the settlers' ultimate turn to struggle *against* an imperial power, rather than their history of sponsorship by it, that becomes ensconced as the national narrative.

The UN Partition was the second promise, resulting from attempts by the "world community," in the form of the very newly created United Nations, to figure out how to deal with Palestine. By 1947, the British were sick of their mandate, and they couldn't get rid of it fast enough. They handed their problem over to the UN. In one of its early major decisions, the UN decided to partition the British mandate of Palestine into two states, plus an international zone comprising Jerusalem and Bethlehem.

We can see the creation of these states as a promise: the UN would support the formation of self-determination and independent states for these two peoples. We might also understand why Israel embraced that promise (even though most Zionists hoped for the entire territory). Palestinians and nearby Arab states, on the other hand, saw the division of their land as another form of imperialism. They argued that neither the United Nations nor anyone else had the right to deny them self-determination in land where they were the Indigenous majority.

Even if one accepted partition, the split certainly was not equitable relative to the population. The proposed Jewish state covered 56% of Mandatory Palestine although Jews were only one third of the total population; the Arab state covered 43% of the territory. The Arab state was supposed to be linked to the separate British protectorate of Transjordan.

Civil war broke out almost immediately after the UN's official vote for partition in November 1947, as Arab and Jewish militias attacked each other and fought for territory. The Zionist military organizations were highly effective, and more than

700,000 Palestinian residents fled or were expelled. (It was during this time that Darwish and his family left to Lebanon, before secretly returning after the war's end.) By the time Israel declared its independence in May of 1948, the Palestinians had been largely defeated. Nearby Arab states (Egypt, Syria, Jordan, and Iraq) entered the war to prevent further displacement and to stop the partition if they could. This is the moment we often hear about, when the leaders of Arab states were said to have threatened to "drive Israel into the sea." The evidence of that particular threat is contested, but there is no doubt that the Arab side wanted what the Israeli side also wanted: to grab as much of the partitioned land as they could. It was a house-by-house, village-by-village struggle to gain territory for self-rule.[65]

There is much to say about the viciousness of some of those battles, but the point here is to understand what each side hoped for: what their horizon of the future looked like. Both saw the war as a chance to control a home space, to grab or keep land for inhabitation and to build a political system around the land they held. Arab armies were defeated within a few months, and when the fighting stopped, Israeli forces had extended their control over territory, so that Israel now covered 78% of historic Palestine. Arab states then divided up what was left. Jordan annexed what came to be called the West Bank and tried hard to eradicate any separate Palestinian identity. (Britain and Pakistan were the only countries that recognized Jordan's annexation.) Egypt took control of Gaza but considered it to be Palestinian territory under Egypt's temporary administration. (In the 1967 war, Israel would conquer both Gaza and the West Bank, as well Sinai and the Golan.)

Thus the promise of two states was a promise ultimately delivered only to Israel. Some historians say that the lack of a Palestinian state today is because of the original Arab opposition to Partition. It makes sense to me, though, that Arab residents of Palestine were unwilling to accept what they saw as the imposition of a sovereign state in their homeland—that they had seen the UN promise as a theft. The 1948 war left their situation profoundly diminished. Many had been expelled from their homes or had fled and now were living in refugee camps—in the West Bank and Gaza, or in Jordan or Lebanon. Millions of Palestinians remain in those camps to this day. They refuse to "settle" into the 22% of the original Palestine that was left for Palestinians to live in. Some still carry the keys to their old family houses around their neck.

Today, millions of Palestinians are scattered into a global diaspora: living and working in the Gulf states, Europe, or the United States. The Palestinians who could leave the camps or their homes were often those with education and resources. After the 1948 Nakba, displaced Palestinians often ended up in Kuwait or the United Arab Emirates, where they came to make up a significant percentage of teachers and bureaucrats. (By the 1970s, nearly 40% of the available labor force in the West Bank and Gaza was employed in Arab countries.)[66] Palestinians moved to Europe and the US as well. Mahmoud Darwish spent many years in Paris. In London today, the Palestinian arts community is thriving: the "first lady of Arabic hip hop," Shadia Mansour, lives there, as does the installation artist Mona Hatoum. In the US, there are Palestinian contingents in every city with a large Arab American population: Detroit and Dearborn, New York, Los Angeles, Chicago, and Washington, DC.[67] But Palestinians are also dispersed into many other parts of the country: back in the 1990s, the best Italian restaurant in Boston's North End was run by a Palestinian; the best-selling novelist Etaf Rum lives in a small town in eastern North Carolina.

The last of the three promises was the Oslo Accords, signed in 1993. After a long series of secret negotiations, the PLO and the government of Israel agreed to recognize each other. The talks achieved some tangible, hopeful outcomes: the PLO's recognition of Israel, and Israel's agreement to withdraw its military forces from some of the territory it had occupied since 1967, particularly Jericho in the West Bank and all of Gaza except near the Jewish settlements.[68] The PLO leadership would be allowed to return to the West Bank, which, for individuals who had been exiled for decades, was a crucial victory.

The harder issues were all pushed down the road for the "final status" negotiations to come: Jewish settlements, borders, the return of Palestinian refugees, and the status of Jerusalem. The promise of Oslo, in the words of its declaration, was that the two sides would "strive to live in peaceful co-existence and mutual dignity and security and achieve a just, lasting, and comprehensive settlement."[69]

That didn't happen. Was it ever even possible under Oslo's framework? At the time, many people thought it was. American Jewish peace activist Wendy Orange was living in Israel in the early 1990s and has written powerfully about the joy and hope she felt. She was in Jerusalem when the accords were announced, and she describes poring over the text of the agreement, which in her view outlined "how and when the Palestinians will take control over their own lives." She couldn't believe that the peace she and others had worked toward and dreamed about was now public policy. In her crowd, "every conversation is high-pitched with exhilaration."[70] There were doubters. Many key Palestinian leaders who had lived and organized in the West Bank and Gaza for decades feared that they would be pushed aside now that the PLO officials were coming back.

A friend of Orange also warned her that Gazans were generally more suspicious of such deals: they tended to be more radical, more wary of the Palestinian leadership abroad. Yet, as others have documented, the night before the accords were to be officially signed, Gazans drove down the streets in trucks, joyously waving Palestinian flags, shouting "Gaza and Jericho first!" A few months later, when most of Israel's troops did indeed pull out of Gaza, people started to come out on the streets at night, just to walk around in public—to feel free.[71]

There were a number of Palestinians, however, who thought the Oslo process not just a dead end, but that it was designed to be that way. Israel had recognized the PLO but had made no promise of a Palestinian state. The historian Rashid Khalidi, who had been part of earlier negotiations in Washington, argues that what the PLO had agreed to "was a highly restricted form of self-rule in a fragment of the Occupied Territories, and without control of land, water, borders, or much else."[72] The Oslo Accords created the Palestinian Authority (PA), which seemed to be a step forward. The PA had joint control with Israel over security in parts of the West Bank, and would also control some internal functions, such as schools. But the PA did not and does not have *sovereignty* over anything, including its own taxes (which are collected by Israel and then transferred back).

The future steps toward the "final status" negotiation never moved forward significantly because the two sides had essentially signed different agreements. The PLO leadership interpreted "autonomy" as a stepping-stone to a fully realized state in the West Bank and Gaza. The Israelis saw autonomy as something that could be increased over time—more of the West Bank under PA authority, more responsibility over particular sectors—but not transformed into eventual sovereignty. In 1995, just two years after he had signed the Accords, Prime Minister Yitzhak Rabin told the Israeli Knesset openly that any Palestinian "entity" that did emerge from Oslo would be "less than a state."[73] (Later that year, he was assassinated by a right-wing law student who had opposed the terms of the Oslo Accords.)

Upon learning of the details of the Accords, the great Palestinian American scholar Edward Said called Oslo "an instrument of Palestinian surrender."[74] Said resigned his role on the Palestinian National Council in protest, while Darwish resigned from the PLO Executive Committee.

OCTOBER 26

I remember a conversation I once had with my friend Amira, a colleague I've known since we were both in grad school. It was sometime around 2008. Oslo was still limping along, and, as part of that process, Palestine had held legislative elections in 2006—which, to the shock of many, Hamas had won, running on a platform of anti-corruption and good governance. Outside observers were surprised at Hamas's showing, even though, for people like Amira, signs of the outcome had been evident for some time. She had grown up on the West Bank in the 1970s and 1980s. She was a member of the Communist Party, which, unlike other Palestinian groups or the Arab states, recognized Israel and supported a two-state solution. (Mahmoud Darwish had been a member of Israel's Communist Party in his day.) My friend was a nationalist activist, hanging out with a largely leftist, educated, secular Palestinian movement that was emerging in relation to, but separate from, the PLO, whose leadership was based in Tunis.

By the time of the 2006 elections, the Palestinian Authority was cheek-by-jowl with Israel, serving essentially as the subcontractor for Israel's rule over the West Bank and Gaza. The PA, and Fatah—its dominant faction—were widely seen as corrupt and hapless, having sold out the hopes of the Oslo Accords for the job of managing a neutered "non-state" in the West Bank and Gaza.

In a complicated series of events following the Hamas victory, Fatah and Hamas initially formed a governing coalition, which soon broke down; Fatah tried to take control of both the West Bank and Gaza in what was essentially a coup. There was fighting on the streets in Gaza, a battle that Fatah lost. The election was "nulled" in the West Bank, but Hamas got Gaza. This would lead to the imposition of a certain form of Islamic law in Gaza, but also to the emergence of Hamas as an actual government, one that tried to provide hospitals and services while also engaging in rhetorical grand gestures and the occasional attack on Israeli targets.

Immediately after Hamas took control of Gaza, Israel—supported by Egypt—imposed a blockade on movement and goods out of the territory. The blockade, which kept most people in and most goods out, lasted for more than 16 years: it began in 2007, when Hamas took power and Israel's cabinet classified Gaza as a "hostile entity." The blockade prohibited imports of all but 18 "basic goods" into Gaza, banned all exports, and prevented international aid agencies from having any working contact with Hamas—the de facto government. This meant that food and medical aid, when it was allowed in, had to be delivered directly by the NGOs, bypassing the existing hospitals or social service programs. Long-term development work was all but impossible. By 2020, Gaza's unemployment rate was one of the highest in the world, its GDP per capita was one-fourth that of the West Bank, and 64% of its population was food insecure.[75]

Once Hamas assumed rule over Gaza, it, along with other armed groups, intermittently fired missiles into Israel—thousands of them over the years. Israel often responded with bombs or missiles of its own. Israel also launched larger military campaigns against Hamas in 2008, 2012, and, most significantly, in 2014, when approximately 2,000 Palestinians were killed.[76] Israel was focused primarily on maintaining the Strip's marginalization, its separation from the West Bank, and its invisibility in the daily lives of most Israelis. Asked what

Israeli policy toward Gaza was in the 2010s, an IDF official responded with just seven words: "No development, no prosperity, no humanitarian crisis."[77]

Looking back on Hamas's rise, Amira told me about how, sometime during the early 1980s, these new Islamist guys had started showing up, the precursors of Hamas. They seemed so ridiculous, she said, quoting the Quran and demanding Islamic law. They spent their time in the mosque or studying, not doing any real political work. Meanwhile, her secular cohort continued their activism—the first Intifada began a few years later in 1987, a peaceful uprising of Palestinian civil society that seemed, for a time, as if it might shake the Israel occupation to its foundations.

"We just made fun of them and laughed," Amira said about the Islamists. "But we're not laughing now."

OCTOBER 27

My friend David isn't the only one making comparisons between the Hamas attacks and 9/11. They are everywhere in the US media. There are some clear reasons for that: the perpetrators are Islamists and the majority of victims civilian.[78] The numbers of dead and injured are high, but not so high as to be uncountable. The Israeli victims' names and life stories have been in the media, both in Israel and here in the US.

However, there are crucial differences between the attacks that can't be overlooked: between Al-Qaeda and Hamas, and between Bin Laden's vision of a global caliphate and Hamas's dream of a Palestinian homeland. Al-Qaeda was cult-like, driven by a global apocalyptic vision but rooted nowhere. Hamas, by contrast, is deeply rooted: an elected governing authority. Its members are involved in a range of local activities, from garbage collection to medicine—not just guerilla or violent action. (And, as is the case with most governments, many of those governed by Hamas in Gaza do not support everything it does.)

In addition, Netanyahu's immediate launch of the war on Gaza took away the chance for Israelis and Jews around the world—and, really, all of us—to process the horror of the Hamas attack. Israel's massive bombing campaign over the last weeks has meant that, from the outset, discussions of the October 7 attacks necessarily included some account of Israel's devastating and indiscriminate bombing of the people of Gaza. A murderous rampage by Hamas has been immediately subsumed into the all-out war that we witness today.

Nonetheless, much of the narration of this war has been shaped by the Israeli state's strategic logic and imperatives. A hegemonic discourse emerges, both in Israel and the US: you are either pro-Hamas or anti-Hamas; pro-Israel or anti-Israel. You support the war or you support the terrorists. To say that this is Israel's 9/11 seems to be a way of saying that the war against Gaza is righteous, in the same way that (for a time at least) the US war in Afghanistan was treated by much of the international community as justified. The murdered victims of Hamas's terror will be held innocent, whereas those other deaths—those of Palestinians—will be blamed on Hamas itself, for its resistance against the blockade of Gaza, and for its embeddedness in the territory it governed. Hamas is fighting a guerilla war in populated areas, which means that Israel will claim they are using civilians as "shields."

Perhaps Netanyahu wanted exactly this: to preclude the possibility of a deep sorrow and anger in Israel that did not immediately reach for violence; to foreclose the prospect of imagining a different way forward, or at least a more limited response.

Beyond Israel's borders, however, the narrative has played out differently. The Israeli public may not be focusing on the Palestinian dead, but much of the rest of the world has been—

and the numbers skew very quickly. Indeed, for some of the people I know or who I follow on social media, the great disparities of the dead and injured and homeless make it difficult to acknowledge Israel's loss at all.

But perhaps it is possible to refuse the state's logic altogether: to genuinely mourn civilians on all sides, and to do so without losing sight of the historical contexts of oppression and the real differences in power as that is evidenced on the ground.

I keep thinking back to one of my favorite works of art about September 11, a long piece called "First Writing Since" by Palestinian American poet Suheir Hammad.[79] In it, Hammad articulates her own complex position as a New Yorker, a Palestinian, a critic of US empire, and a person who also refuses to shut her eyes to the death and destruction of 9/11. Her poem begins this way:

> there have been no words.
> i have not written one word.
> no poetry in the ashes south of canal
> street.
> no prose in the refrigerated trucks
> driving debris and dna
> not one word.[80]

Not one word. She is there in New York, silenced by the "debris and dna." The poet goes on, describing New York's streets, the mix of people. She imagines all the silent "thank yous" of those who just missed being in the towers: "thank you for my lazy procrastinating ass. thank you to the germs that had me call in sick." She describes hearing a sobbing woman in a car. Hammad starts to reach out to her but then hears the woman talking to herself: "we're gonna burn them so bad, i swear, so bad." And she realizes that "them" is actually her, or at least people who look like her.

For me the most powerful moment in the poem is when Hammad complains about the quick emergence of leftist commentary about US culpability. This is blowback, her political allies were saying. Don't forget what the US has done in the Middle East. There are reasons why Al-Qaeda saw the US as an aggressor, as an empire. Hammad doesn't disagree, but, she says:

> hold up with that, cause i live here,
> these are my friends and fam, and it
> could have been me in those
> buildings, and we're not bad people,
> do not support america's bullying.
> can I just have a half second to feel
> bad?

She seems to ask, first, for the time to mourn. The poem goes on to describe the flyers that are pasted everywhere in New York, saying "please help us find George," or "Priti," or my "sister girl." Walking around the city, Hammad finds herself crying in the arms of a white woman on the street.

Later, the poet does indeed get angry, cursing. We see how her fury rises when people assume that she represents all Arabs, or that "Arabs" are evil. When they act as if no Arabs or Muslims died in the towers. Hammad goes on to critique US international power, racism, and the politics of post-9/11 American nationalism with precise cuts.

Indeed, it wasn't long before the FBI began to round up Arabs and Muslims for "interviews." Anti-Muslim and anti-Arab sentiment increased dramatically; in the streets and at workplaces, people who "looked Arab" or women who covered their hair were harassed and even killed.[81] Soon the US prepared to launch not one war, but two, each of which would leave unimagined devastation in its wake. Looking back on those wars, Brown University's Costs of War project has estimated that 900,000 people were killed directly by the post-9/11 wars (primarily in Iraq and Afghanistan), while another 3.5 million died from indirect causes such as malnutrition and disease.[82]

But Hammad cannot know any of that in the first weeks after the September 11 attacks. She was aware—we all were—of the threat of war, the realpolitik of American power. But her poem ends differently, with a claim that perhaps only a young person—or a poet—could pull off. Recognizing all the horror, the political failures that led to September 11, and even the likely wars to come, she nonetheless arrives at this:

> affirm life.
> affirm life.
> we got to carry each other now.
> you are either with life, or against it.
> affirm life.

On March 7, 2009, I saw Suheir Hammad perform to a packed audience at the Kennedy Center's Millennium Stage in Washington, DC. She gave an electric reading from a new series of poems, each named after a city in Gaza. An hour or so later, Marcel Khalife and the Al Mayadine Ensemble performed on the main stage. The evening's performance was titled "And We Love Life. . . A Salute to Mahmoud Darwish."[83]

OCTOBER 28

Israel began its full-scale invasion of Gaza today. Tanks and other armored vehicles rolled into the strip from the north and east. The attacks from air and sea have not ended, but now thousands of soldiers (Israel isn't saying how many) are poised for close combat with Hamas and other fighters. All electricity and cell service in Gaza is cut. There is very little other information, but Israel reports having confronted and killed several "terrorists."[84]

OCTOBER 29

One summer evening in the early 1990s, before Oslo, I was talking to my friend Sohaib about whether a two-state solution was likely, or even possible. We had become friends through our activism, over the course of countless meetings, which involved many arguments over what statements to issue, what protest signs to make. The specific plan of choice differed by group and individual; we would spend hours crafting flyers in order to come to wording on the future status of Jerusalem or the role of the UN. Sohaib was politically active with various Palestinian groups, and so we ran in some of the same circles: a mélange of Arab American activists, anti-interventionist and peace activists, and a small but crucial set of Jewish leftists.

Sohaib was an immigrant and not yet a citizen in the 1980s, I think, and he was energized, like me, by the multiethnic, if still quite small, community that emerged around the Palestinian cause. As we talked, I remember him telling me that he had the "right" to be anti-Jewish: Israeli Jews had taken everything from his family. His grandparents had lived in northern Palestine and had fled in 1948. They traveled on foot to the Palestinian refugee camps in Lebanon. His mother had to carry her little brother. His grandfather carried his own mother on his back, since she was too old and feeble to walk herself. Eventually, his father moved the family from Lebanon to Syria, then to Abu Dhabi. Sohaib came to the Boston area when he was in his twenties, but his politics were shaped by the uprooting of Palestinian life represented by the refugee camps. "Still," Sohaib said, "I'm *not* against Jews. I'm a humanist."

Sohaib was part of the Arab American left, which was central to the fight for Palestinian rights in the United States. Groups such as the Association of Arab American University Graduates and the Palestine Human Rights Campaign might have had differences with each other, but they shared a commitment to seeing Palestine as part of the struggle for Third World liberation more broadly. They insisted that US backing for Israel was, essentially, imperialist: the US was trying to extend its reach in the Middle East (and for this reason managed also to keep Saudi Arabia and Jordan as close allies), while Israel was expanding its hold on Palestinian land literally day by day. This cohort of activists also included groups like the Middle East Philanthropic Fund and the Middle East Children's Fund (both of which sponsored Marcel Khalife's concerts in the 1980s).[85] Intellectuals and writers with MENA heritage were increasingly visible as well: scholars Edward Said and Walid Khalidi, poets Naomi Shihab Nye and Lisa Suhair Majaj, novelist Etel Adnan, among others.

Sohaib and I both knew that, alongside Arab Americans, American Jews had been crucial in bringing Palestine to bear as an issue in left and liberal politics. In the 1970s and 1980s, some Jews on the American left saw Israel-Palestine as their particular burden, at a time when few other people paid attention at all. Jewish feminists led the way, and they showed real guts in jumping in to demand that all those folks who were worried about El Salvador or South Africa, about global feminist solidarity or nuclear war, should also be thinking about what was happening in Israel and the Occupied Territories.

Feminist newspapers in the 1980s were filled with discussions about Palestine, Zionism, and antisemitism. "We are an organization of anti-imperialist women; many of us are Jewish," wrote one group to the American feminist magazine *Sojourner* in 1982. "We are very disturbed at the growing tendency to use the issue of antisemitism to justify Zionism and the colonization of the Palestinian people."[86] These Jewish voices certainly did not represent most Jews, but they did important work in making it possible to talk about Israel among progressives.

The organization New Jewish Agenda formed in 1980, and at Mobe we worked closely with them on Middle East issues. In 1983, New Jewish Agenda called for a freeze on West Bank settlements. The group was Zionist in the sense that it was committed to Israel as a Jewish state "within its 1967 borders." Some of them saw that there had been an injustice in 1948 too, but they believed the horrors of the Holocaust made a specifically Jewish state necessary. They were also fearless, challenging Israeli expansion when most of the Jewish community was hostile to such arguments.

There were also a few Israelis making similar points about the deal-breaking impact of the Jewish settlements. Already in 1982, the former deputy mayor of Jerusalem, Meron Benvenisti, was arguing that Israel should stop the illegal settlements in the Occupied Territories. Not only because they were wrong, but because, in what became almost a mantra, "Israel cannot remain both Jewish and democratic" if it maintained control of the West Bank and Gaza.

That was 41 years ago.[87]

A few months after that summer evening talk, Sohaib asked me how he was supposed to fill out a job application—that part where he had to indicate his "race." Black? Asian? Nothing seemed to fit. I looked at him, brown as toast and bearded, and told him that Arabs are white on the US census. There was a brief silence before he said, "You've gotta be fucking kidding me."[88]

The rush to embrace Israel by most of the American mainstream media is predictable. In my book *Epic Encounters* (2005), I tried to trace the multiple cultural phenomena that had shaped US pro-Israel sentiment: a Christian religious sense of connection to the Holy Land; admiration for Israel's military prowess; a sense of Israeli Jews as "David" in a sea of Arab states. I also argued that US popular culture in the 1950s and 1960s had helped consolidate the pro-Israel sentiments of a generation. Biblical epic films such as *Ben-Hur* (1959) and *The Ten Commandments* (1956) featured Hebrews who faced a despotic state (usually Rome or ancient Egypt, although the rulers always spoke with British accents). At the end of *Ben-Hur*, the friendly old Sheikh, who is providing Ben-Hur's horses in an important race against a Roman soldier, hangs a Star of David necklace over Judah's neck and says to him, "The Star of David—to shine out for your people and my people together, and blind the eyes of Rome!"[89] The film presents Israel as the anti-imperial power that would speak for democracy and freedom, even for Arabs.

In fact, it is hard to imagine a country that has a better on-screen reputation than Israel: burnished by color-saturated Jesus films that seem like ads for Holy Land tourism; celebrated for its little-country-that-could success, as in *Exodus;* or touted for its toughness, as in *Black Sunday* (1977), *Munich* (2005), or *Entebbe* (2018), the fictionalization of Israel's dramatic rescue of passengers on an El Al jet hijacked to Uganda in 1976. While Arabs were presented on screen as terrorists and oil sheiks and terrorists again, Hollywood helped create an image of Israel as "one of us"—not just for Jews, not even primarily for Jews—but for the multi-racial American public that grew up on stories of Israel's valor and righteousness.[90]

My father, who was born in 1934, was a firm Republican white guy who lived his whole life in North Carolina. He was smart as a whip, though he had never gone to college, and he had strong opinions about Israel (amongst many other things). There was one instance I remember when I realized just how far this went. In December 1996, members of the Túpac Amaru Revolutionary Movement in Peru had stormed the house of the Japanese ambassador to Peru during a major diplomatic gathering and took hundreds of hostages. Some were released, but the siege went on for months until Peru eventually launched a successful rescue of the hostages in March of 1997. I was talking on the phone with my father the night of the rescue, listening as he insisted that the Israelis had been intimately involved in helping Peru. I pointed out that it was actually the US that had provided assistance. "No," my father insisted firmly, with no evidence whatsoever. "It was Israel. Because they know how to take care of their people."

NOVEMBER 1

My partner Carl and I talk politics all the time. It's a large part of our lives even in the quietest of times. He is co-director of the Project on Defense Alternatives, which reports on US military policy. He also writes a lot on social media, where he does something I find very difficult: he pays serious attention to multiple global political crises at once. While most people I know (and much of the media) have moved Ukraine to the back burner, Carl continues to follow the devastation and the horrific financial and political costs of that war. He's also on top of the continuing escalation with China, and keeps up with the changing fortunes of Trump's election bid.

Carl has also paid far more attention than I have to the military end of the Gaza war. How many brigades are deployed in Gaza and what are their capacities? What is the military strategy as understood by Israel? We talk frequently about the US supplying weapons to Israel. Israel is already by far the largest recipient of US aid over the last 70 years; today its regular military aid package is close to $4 billion a year.[91] Now the US is also providing the specific equipment that Israel says it needs for the Gaza invasion. (The US weapons industry is thriving with all the conflicts. American manufacturers supply 40% of all global weapons sales.)

Today Carl has posted and commented on an article by Stephen Zunes that argues that Hamas's rise from a small religious party to major player in the Israel-Palestine conflict results from Washington's failure to be an honest broker in the Oslo peace process.[92] Had a genuine Palestinian state been on the table at Oslo, rejectionist groups such as Hamas would likely have been marginalized. It is true that the US has almost never been willing to push Israel. It has refused to use aid or even diplomacy to insist that Israel stop its settlements, the administrative detentions that imprison thousands of Palestinians without trial, or the daily humiliations of occupation. Both the US and Israel have failed to support a deal that included genuine Palestinian sovereignty over the West Bank and Gaza. At the time of Oslo, a lot of people hoped and believed it could happen. The Cold War was over and new possibilities seemed ready to be born.

Tonight over dinner, Carl and I had another of our "What are they thinking" conversations. How can Americans not see how much of a role that uncritical US support for Israel has played in destroying the hopes of Palestinians? And how can the Israeli government, the US government, the Israeli public, and much of the US public *not* see how the utter loss of any hope for genuine Palestinian self-determination is going to lead to more radicalization, not less?

NOVEMBER 4

As of today, 9,485 Gazans have been killed and almost 25,000 injured, according to the UN. Approximately 62% of the population is internally displaced.[93]

This evening, I attended a special panel about Gaza at the Middle East Studies Association meeting. It was at 8 p.m. on a Saturday night: the panel was organized quickly and at a time when conference goers are usually out with friends, eating and chatting. Hundreds of people were there to listen. This was not a crowd that needed Gaza 101. They wanted to hear insider perspectives, to gather with others to think and to feel together. Omar Shakir, the Israel and Palestine Director for Human Rights Watch, gave a presentation that swiftly brought home how bad things are in Gaza. He focused on the bombing deaths and the lack of services: no electricity and little clean water, hospitals collapsing. He is clearly living this every day, every breath. Like the Palestinians I see on Instagram, he seems to wonder whether and how he is going to get people to listen.

One of the most powerful presentations at the panel was by a young Israeli scholar, Shay Hazkani. His remit was to update the group on Israeli public opinion, but he began by saying that it is clear that Hamas committed horrific crimes. He talked about is a video compiled by Israeli officials—some of it taken from the fighters' cameras, some from security footage—that is being shown to journalists and foreign government officials, but not available for general viewing. This footage makes clear that, once the fighters left the music festival and arrived in the various towns nearby, they engaged in a brutal 12-hour slaughter.[94]

Prof. Hazkani went on to remind us that not only do we need to know the full truth, we also need to know specifically what Israelis are being told. Their narratives are not the narratives we have seen in the US press, which itself has been incredibly mixed. Major publications such as the *New York Times* have focused much more on Israeli stories than on Palestinian ones, while other outlets such as *The Nation*, *The Guardian* in the UK, and *Al Jazeera English,* describe what has now become a ground war in Gaza in some detail. There are still no outside journalists being allowed to enter Gaza, so much of what they do report relies on the hard and dangerous work being done by Palestinian journalists.

In any case, Israelis are learning very little of any of that. They know next to nothing about what is happening to civilians in Gaza. They don't want to know. The stories they hear are those of Israeli victims: about the Israeli hostages held somewhere in Gaza, and about those who were killed in the full fury of the October 7 attack—families, young people, fathers, and grandmothers, frightened and suffering through the long unfolding violence. Hazkani told us that the mood in Israel is not tragically sad, although they are mourning. The general sentiment is one of righteous, unmitigated rage. Much of the nation is united around the demand, absolute, for retribution. The killings have led to the collapse of the Israeli left, what there was of it. And the country is polling ever-more rightward.

Israelis still don't love Netanyahu; many blame his government for the security failures that allowed the Hamas attack to happen. But, overall, they do strongly endorse the war.

NOVEMBER 5

The American Studies Association is meeting in Montreal, where yesterday I presented the Marcel Khalife talk I have been working on intermittently for the last two months. In my presentation I tried to unpack what Khalife meant, to Arab American audiences in particular, at a moment of crisis—a moment not dissimilar to the one we are living in. Khalife's first tour in the US was in 1982, just after the Israeli invasion of Lebanon, and the proceeds went to aid victims of the war. He continued to visit every year or two, singing the political songs that made him famous. *Promises of the Storm* was finally released in the US by a tiny left-wing record label in 1983, but the bootleg cassette tapes and multiple tours had already done their work.

I show the YouTube clip of Khalife playing "As I Walk." I talk about how the song is a strange one for such a joyous performance, with Khalife leading and the audience singing along. "As I Walk" tells the story of a person who walks with an olive branch in one hand while carrying his coffin on his shoulder, signaling a readiness to die for the Palestinian cause. The song resonates clearly with a 1974 speech that the former Palestinian President Yasser Arafat gave before the UN, in which he famously said "I have come bearing an olive branch and a freedom fighter's gun. Do not let the olive branch fall from my hand."[95]

That speech was written by Mahmoud Darwish and translated into English by the Palestinian American scholar Edward Said. The song and the speech both demonstrate the tension of carrying a belief in the imminent possibility of peace, alongside a willingness to fight and die for a state that might still be won. In the 1980s, then, there was a vision of a real future for Palestine—one of those "futures past" that has become increasingly hard to recapture, much less imagine as our own.

Another of the panelists, Dr. Sophia Azeb, professor of literature at UC Santa Cruz, pulled out of her presentation to attend a major pro-Palestinian demonstration being held in Montreal. (There was a simultaneous protest in Washington, DC, drawing tens of thousands, at which people carried small paper coffins or white sheets made to look like body bags.[96]) Sophia felt she could not be anywhere other than the demonstration. During the previous week, her family's house on the West Bank had been attacked by settlers who were emboldened by the war on Gaza. The settlers were trying to claim the family's olive trees, and to push her extended family out of their home.

The situation Sophia's family faces has become increasingly common. For years, settlers have been making land grabs, operating with the complicity and sometimes the assistance of the IDF. There had already been a dramatic increase in settler violence in the first half of 2023, with settlers regularly blockading roads, setting cars or homes on fire, burning or cutting down olive trees, and vandalizing churches or mosques. The UN documented three settler incidents a day in September, just before the October 7 attacks. Now the outright seizure of land is becoming more brazen. In recent months, settlers have forced nearly 1,000 Palestinians from their homes.[97]

Every settlement in the West Bank is built on Palestinian land. Before Israel took the territory in 1967, Palestinians owned the land, built their houses, tended their groves, ran their businesses, all while living under Jordanian rule in part of what had been proposed as a Palestinian state in 1947.

Since 1967, however, Israel's rule has been not only about sovereignty but also dispossession. The slow one-sided war Israel has been conducting over the last 50-plus years has been one of inches. Some Palestinians retaliate against settler violence: the day after an Israeli military raid into Jenin in June 2023, for example, Palestinian gunmen killed four Israelis at a restaurant and a gas station near an Israeli settlement.[98] But Palestinians simply do not have the capacity to carry out the kind of systemic violence that Israelis inflict on the West Bank. It is virtually impossible for a Palestinian in the West Bank to steal a settler's land, burn down their house, destroy their business, or build a road that cuts a family off from their income-producing olive groves. Every gain of territory is gained by Israelis; every home or business destroyed is taken from Palestinians.

NOVEMBER 6

I just listened to Omar Baddar's interview with the podcaster Krystal Kyle. Baddar, a Palestinian American journalist and policy analyst, recently wrote an essay for *Newsweek* calling out the double-standard applied to Palestinians: "No one believes that Hamas's indiscriminate attack on Israeli military and civilian targets on October 7 was a legitimate response to what Israel has done. So why is Israel's bombing of Gazans not only not condemned, but actively supported?"[99]

By now, with many more thousands dead, he is even sharper in his critique. He tells Kyle that "what Israel is engaged in right now in Gaza is a massive campaign of terrorism [...] And we have a situation in which US policy is to cover for this massive campaign of terrorism in the name of fighting terrorism, ironically."[100]

You can hear his frustration, his mounting anger—which is what I also feel among friends and colleagues. Outrage and despair are joined with a feeling of helplessness, of being utterly incapable of making a difference. Yet I also feel the privilege in my distance from the suffering in Gaza now. Despite my attention to the news, the fact is that I *can* turn away and eat a good meal or watch a movie. The people in Gaza have no such options. The death toll in the enclave is just over 10,000. 40% are children.

NOVEMBER 8

It's been just over a month since the Hamas attack. The leaders of the organization have been withering under Israeli assault, and an unknown number of them have been killed. But that's not necessarily all bad for Hamas. Writing for the Center for Strategic and International Studies, a moderately conservative US think tank, Jon Alterman argues that Israel's violence is giving Hamas the political advantage:

Hamas sees victory not in one year or five, but from engaging with decades of struggle that increase Palestinian solidarity and increase Israel's isolation. In this scenario, Hamas rallies a besieged population in Gaza around it in anger and helps collapse the Palestinian Authority government by ensuring Palestinians see it even more as a feckless adjunct to Israeli military authority. Meanwhile, Arab states move strongly away from normalization, the Global South aligns strongly with the Palestinian cause, Europe recoils at the Israeli army's excesses, and an American debate erupts over Israel, destroying the bipartisan support Israel has enjoyed here since the early 1970s. Rumblings of a regional war suit Hamas well, prompting global debates about the cost of an alliance with Israel. Israel's ability to sustain its own solidarity through this process is not Hamas' main concern. Rather, its goal is to estrange Israel from its international partners and turn it into the pariah that Hamas believes it to be.[101]

This is clearly happening. Support for Israel's war against Gaza is rapidly declining globally. And people around the world are asking questions about why Palestinians are *still* so vulnerable to Israeli bombardment. Hamas does indeed have increased support in Gaza. In the summer of 2023, only 30% of Gazans said they supported Hamas, blaming the governing party for economic problems, inefficiency, and the lack of progress toward ending the occupation of Gaza.[102] After the October 7 attacks, however, and in the wake of sustained Israeli bombardment, 59% of Palestinians in Gaza said they viewed Hamas "very" or "somewhat" positively.[103] That might change, if the war continues in this vein. At some point, Hamas may come to be seen by Gazans as both the instigator of this wildly disproportionate war and as a force too weak to protect its population. Or perhaps not. When faced with this truly unparalleled level of violence—more bombs dropped than in any other twenty-first century conflict—then it also makes sense that those who gain legitimacy among Palestinians are those who fight back.

NOVEMBER 9

More than 750 journalists from a broad range of media outlets have signed a letter saying that newsrooms are "accountable for dehumanizing rhetoric that has served to justify ethnic cleansing of Palestinians." They argue that newsrooms have systemically undermined Palestinian, Arab, and Muslim perspectives, dismissing them as "unreliable." And that they have, since October 7, written about the Hamas attack as the starting point of the conflict rather than part of a much longer and broader struggle—one that centers on Israel's long control over Palestinian territories and the horrific conditions and dehumanization experienced by the population of Gaza.[104]

Much of the letter also focuses on the fact that so many journalists have been killed. They describe the airstrike that killed the wife and children of Wael Al-Dahdouh, *Al Jazeera*'s Gaza bureau chief, and a November 5 strike on the home of journalist Mohammed Abu Hasira that killed him and 42 family members. So far at least 26 journalists have been killed.

NOVEMBER 10

The Guardian reports today that both Islamophobia and antisemitism have sharply increased in the United States since the start of the war. In terms of Arabs and Muslims, this is not surprising: conflicts in the Middle East have often resonated in the US, stoking racism. There was anti-Arab sentiment during the oil shocks of the 1970s, attacks on Iranians in the US during the hostage crisis of 1979–80, images of Palestinians as terrorists in the 1980s and Muslims as terrorists after September 11. Just last month, the Council on American-Islamic Relations (CAIR) noted a 216% increase in reports of bias against Muslims or Arabs compared to the same period last year. This included hateful rhetoric, silencing, and violence, including murder and attempted murder.[105]

Antisemitism is also on the rise. In the last few decades, virulent forms of antisemitism and conspiracy theory have often been associated with the rise of the alt-right in both Europe and the US. In Europe, in particular, the alt-right's antisemitism is often tied to anti-Muslim and anti-immigrant sentiment—all wrapped up into one white supremacist package.[106] In 2020, Pew Research was already showing a rise in antisemitic incidents across 94 countries; a 2018 poll by CNN found that more than 25% of Europeans believed that Jews had too much power in finance and business.[107]

In just the last month, the Anti-Defamation League (ADL) has reported a nearly 400% increase in antisemitic incidents from the same period last year. Unlike Pew, however, the ADL includes certain forms of political speech about Israel in its definition. Of the ADL's 312 reported incidents over the last month, 109 occurred at "anti-Israel" rallies, where, the organization says, there was "either strong implicit support for Hamas and/or violence against Jews in Israel."[108]

Definitions matter here. While hostility, violence, or threats of violence against Jews clearly should be categorized as antisemitism (and these are unquestionably on the rise), a number of commentators and politicians are increasingly treating certain criticisms of Israel as inherently antisemitic.[109] Groups such as the ADL and, more recently, the US House of Representatives, draw on a widely circulated definition of antisemitism put forward by the organization International Holocaust Resource Awareness (IHRA). That definition is simple, but the examples that are attached to it are deeply problematic. While IHRA explicitly states that *not* all criticism of Israel is *inherently* antisemitic, it argues that certain types of criticisms of Zionism or Israel are necessarily so. That is, one is allowed to criticize specific Israeli policies or the Israeli prime minister or the Jewish settlements, but not the fundamental dispossession of Palestinians at the heart of the Israeli state.

The IHRA's examples of antisemitism include anything that suggests that "the existence of Israel is racist" or anything that "appl[ies] double-standards" to Israel by requiring "behavior not expected or demanded by any other democratic nation."[110] A number of organizations and individual American Jews have challenged these claims, saying that the conflation of Israel with Jews overall makes it harder to actually identify the real threats that Jews in the US and Europe face: from murders in synagogues to quotidian discrimination and hostility.[111]

For me, as an American Studies professor, it can seem strange that the first of these examples—about acknowledging

Israel's foundation in ethnic exclusivity—is up for debate at all. My work requires that I operate with a deep awareness of the fundamental dispossession of Indigenous peoples that accompanied US settlement, as well as the profound racialized violence of slavery that underwrote American and global capitalism. Similarly, a number of scholars and activists have long criticized the fundamental premises of Zionism. This includes a whole generation of New Historians in Israel, who, starting in the 1980s, made careful, scholarly arguments about the violence and forced displacements of Palestinians in 1948.[112] Acknowledgement of difficult truths over nationalist myths is part of the creation of a truly open and democratic public sphere, one not tied to the needs or interests of the state per se. And yet the assertion that anti-Zionism equals antisemitism is gaining traction in the US press, as well as among politicians both Democratic and Republican.

The second problematic example from the IHRA is the argument that one should not hold Israel up to a standard not applied to other "democratic states." This makes an interesting assumption about the kind of critique that "democratic states" are actually subject to, and it ignores the fact that criticisms of states are made in a very broad public sphere—one that is cacophonous, declamatory, contradictory, and capacious. Around the world, and certainly in the US, there are harsh comments being made about Israel that *are* also made about other countries, including the United States, every day—statements that call countries imperial powers, fundamentally racist, or killers of children, for example. But when such comments refer to Israel, they are often branded as unfair, as an antisemitic attack. The insistence that such strongly worded critiques of the Israeli state are presumptively antisemitic amounts to nothing less than a demand that Israel, because it claims to represent the world's Jews, should in practice be exempt from the kind of ordinary judgments that other states are in fact subject to.

It is clear to me that this Israeli exception is perilous. We must protect the right to issue judgments, even denunciations, of any state and any policy as necessary to the processes of democratic world-building that is at the heart of any hope for our human future. But it is in these moments of my intense frustration with the Israeli exception that I hold tight to what I have long believed: that any of us who support Palestine and who are not Jewish must always remember the ongoing significance of the Holocaust, a generational trauma that has shaped both American Jewish views of Israel and Israel's own narrative about itself. The Holocaust was underwritten by hundreds of years of anti-Jewish persecution, across many political formations, with hatred and violence against Jews woven into the fabric of daily life in multiple cultures and time periods. The lessons of the Holocaust have almost been cheapened by becoming middle-school talking points, but its victims are still here: the children and grandchildren and great-grandchildren of people who were murdered or incarcerated at the camps are working in your office, hanging out at the dog park. For many Jews, in Israel or around the world, the feeling of precarity is well justified. In Europe and the United States, that can be heightened by the sense that many of their fellow citizens simply don't take antisemitism that seriously.

We have to be clear that opposing antisemitism strongly is not just a moral requirement, although it is. It is also a form of "never again to anyone" politics—a part of remembering what fascism was and is, what it wrought in Europe, and against millions of people. With the alt-right on the rise globally, we cannot place this in the past. At the Unite the Right rally in Charlottesville, Virginia, in 2017, white supremacists showed up carrying Nazi flags and marched the streets chanting "The Jews will not replace us."[113]

NOVEMBER 12

Pro-Palestinian marchers have gathered in cities all over the world during the last week. In London yesterday, police estimated that 300,000 people marched from Hyde Park to the US embassy, carrying Palestinian flags and "Free Palestine" signs. It was a peaceful and energetic march; the only violence was by far-right counter-protesters.[114] There were similar marches yesterday in Brussels, with more than 20,000 people, as well as in Karachi, Berlin, Edinburgh, and Baghdad.[115]

In New York, about 2,000 protestors marched through the city, at points snarling traffic. Many people in the march seemed to have family connections to the region, but others were there simply to protest what they saw as a fundamental injustice. "I have no ties to Palestine other than just basic [...] standing up for human rights," one protestor told a reporter.[116] In Paris, thousands joined a pro-Palestine march yesterday calling for an immediate ceasefire in Gaza. (A pointedly timed march against antisemitism was held in Paris today, with as many as 18,000 people from across the political spectrum, including far-right leader Marine Le Pen.[117])

Protests like this have been happening for the last month. In the United States, at least, they bring together a broad group of people: young and old, many whose families are from the Middle East and North Africa, as well as American Jews, and many others including Latinx, white, Black, and Asian people. There is monumentality to it; a sense of people coming together to do something important and right at a historical moment. Often the signs are straightforward: "Ceasefire Now!" "Free Palestine!" "Let Gaza Live!" There is a feeling of release, of hope, even as things seem more and more dire in Gaza.

There is also controversy. In particular, there is debate over one particular chant: "From the river to the sea, Palestine will be free." The river is the Jordan, the sea is the Mediterranean. The space in between was British Mandatory Palestine. Many hear those words as something far more than a criticism of Israel's policies; they hear a call to get rid of Israel and all the Jews living in it. Both the American Jewish Committee and the Anti-Discrimination League have said that any use of the phrase by Palestinians or their supporters denies Jewish rights to self-determination or calls for the ethnic cleansing of Jews.

At different times, there certainly has been language coming from both Palestinian leaders and the rest of the Middle East that declared that there was no place for Jewish sovereignty and perhaps no place for Jews at all in Palestine. This is true of the 2017 Hamas charter, which, while notably less militant than the original, makes clear in multiple ways that Hamas does not accept Israel's sovereignty over any part of Palestine:

> The expulsion and banishment of the Palestinian people from their land and the establishment of the Zionist entity therein do not annul the right of the Palestinian people to their entire land and do not entrench any rights therein for the usurping Zionist entity.[118]

(A number of experts have, however, convincingly argued that Hamas has at times made clear that it would accept a two-state solution in practice, while rhetorically maintaining its ideological stance that all of Palestine belongs to Palestinians.[119])

Many of the pro-Palestinian protestors insist that "From the river to the sea" has nothing to do with a displacement of Jewish Israelis. It has multiple layers but, they argue, it is mostly simply a call to remember the long history of Palestinian displacement all the way back to 1948, and the fact that they, the Palestinians, are not going away.[120] Still, there is no denying that the "from the river to the sea" does *not* sound like a call for a two-state solution. I would argue its prevalence at the protests is evidence of the rapid decomposition of that imaginative horizon.

There is, we should remember, another version of this phrase. In 1977, the Israel's ruling right-wing Likud Party wrote into its charter:

> The right of the Jewish people to the land of Israel is eternal and indisputable [...] therefore, Judea and Samaria will not be handed to any foreign administration; between the Sea and the Jordan there will only be Israeli sovereignty.[121]

Only Israeli sovereignty between the sea and the Jordan. Certainly Palestinians have no doubt of what that posited about their own hopes for genuine statehood.

At this point, maybe the "river to sea" slogans should be understood not as aspirational so much as descriptive. As several of my colleagues from George Washington University recently argued in *Foreign Affairs* magazine, there is already a "one-state reality." Netanyahu's government makes no secret of its commitment to a single state "in which the law enshrines Jewish supremacy over all Palestinians who remain there."[122] These writers argue that there is, in effect, already one unequal state, built via all the quotidian ways that Israel controls ingress and egress, water rights, land rights, the building of more and more settlements, even the sole right to policing in the largest segment of the West Bank (Area C). If Palestinians are to be free, it will necessarily be within territory that Israel now effectively, if not fully, controls.

NOVEMBER 13

                                                        Almost 100 US State Department employees sign internal memos to Secretary of State Antony Blinken expressing serious concerns about the Biden administration's hands-off position on Israel's increasingly deadly military campaign in Gaza.[123]

It's about time. One of the most striking things about all the protests and activity in the US is how little focus there has been on US government policy. Israel is already a major recipient of US military aid and now the US is throwing more money and weapons its way. The Biden administration is proposing an additional $14.3 billion in military aid for the Gaza war. The Israeli Defense Forces already use US-made arms, such as M-113A armored personnel carriers, 155mm artillery shells, and massive 2,000-pound bombs.[124]

This military support is rushed to Israel as both of Gaza's largest hospitals are shut down by a lack of electricity. Doctors at Al-Shifa hospital refuse a mandatory evacuation order, saying that almost 700 patients will die if left behind. Premature babies are being wrapped in foil and placed near hot water in desperate attempts to keep them alive. Over the last five weeks, 11,200 Palestinians have been killed by Israeli attacks.[125]

One can hardly overstate the horror of what is happening. Some of the people being forced out of their homes in Gaza are part of families who lost their homes in 1948, and who lost the world as they knew it when Israel took Gaza in 1967. The world, and particularly the US, has shown a stunning level of disinterest in the multiple and quotidian ways that Palestinian lives under Israeli rule have been increasingly structured to be unlivable.

Today, there is less and less excuse for not knowing exactly what that unlivability looks like. On Instagram or other social media, both professional journalists and ordinary people in Palestine are documenting live the trauma they are experiencing. They take videos of destroyed buildings or people in line for food, and offer commentary, often personal, uploading their videos when they finally get internet access. Hind Khoudary is a freelance journalist who reports with courage and heart. A few days ago, she uploaded a one-month montage on her Instagram account, including scenes of carnage on the streets, people crying in hospitals, her crying with an older woman in her arms. There is one remarkable shot of her high up on some rubble, looking over a large area of damaged buildings and explaining, almost yelling, that there is a line of people down there trying to help a man extract his young son from one of the destroyed buildings. Khoudary's large brown eyes are expressive, and she is almost always in motion. But sometimes, she just sits silently, overwhelmed.[126]

NOVEMBER 14
Thousands of people gather for a pro-Israel rally on the National Mall in DC, listening to an across-the-aisles line up of US senators and representatives speak of their support for Israel and its war in Gaza. The president of Israel, Isaac Herzog, speaks by video.

Although the sponsorship is Jewish organizations, many of the crowd are evangelical Christians—not surprising, given that conservative white evangelicals are the largest base of support for Israel in the US. Along with Donald Trump and Chuck Schumer, John Hagee was on stage. Hagee, a founder of Christians United for Israel, is a television preacher who has claimed God sent Hitler in order to open the way for the creation of a Jewish State.[127]

Hagee is here for a reason. American Jews are important in advocating for US support of Israel, but conservative white evangelicals are the most significant constituency influencing a pro-Israel US policy. Their reasons for support vary. Hagee is firmly in the prophecy camp—those who believe that Israel is central to God's plan for the Second Coming of Jesus in the end-times. The popularity of prophecy-talk ebbs and flows with political events, but it's had a good run since the start of the war. TBN, the Pentecostal-oriented Christian network, has broadcast a plethora of shows issuing dire warnings about the various signs of the end times to be detected in current events. This is not new; a certain strand of evangelicalism has been finding these resonances since the nineteenth century, and their enthusiasm escalated dramatically with the founding of Israel in 1948 and again in the wake of the 1967 war.[128] At the turn of the twenty-first century, and especially after September 11, a set of evangelical novels called the *Left Behind* series kept popping up on the *New York Times* bestseller list, written by an intrepid prophecy-watcher named Tim LaHaye who teamed up with a fiction writer to turn the end-times into an action adventure, with Israelis among its most important heroes.[129]

Other conservative evangelicals support Israel with equal fervor, however, without being particularly interested in planning for the end-times. Evangelicals read what Christians call the Old Testament carefully, and they believe that Jews (or maybe just Israeli Jews) are indeed God's chosen people. They also travel to Israel on Holy Land tours (as do many other types of Christians), where they listen to Israeli guides offering carefully crafted touristic narratives that posit Israel as the caretaker of key parts of Christian history.[130] These conservative evangelicals far outnumber American Jews, and they use their power at the polls to elect candidates who are not just pro-Israel but strong supporters of the Israeli right.[131]

At rallies like the one in DC today, Jews and Christians who agree on little else—neither the nature of faith nor many aspects of domestic politics—are united around Israel. The organizers render a clean formula: If you love Israel, you love Jews; if you care about Jews, you care about Israel.

Walter Benjamin famously wrote that to articulate the past historically does not mean "to recognize it 'the way it really was.'" Rather, he argues, understanding the past requires that we "seize hold of a memory as it flashes up in a moment of danger." We grasp our memories to keep us true to both past realities and future dreams. The danger and the threat for Benjamin is blind conformism, which is different from the genuine traditions that might bind people together. Writing in 1940, as he was fleeing the Nazi conformism of Vichy France, Benjamin argued that "in every era the attempt must be made anew to wrest tradition from a conformism that is about to overpower it."[132]

Conformism versus tradition meant specific things for Benjamin, but for me, for now, the tradition worth holding onto is the belief that Palestinians can and must have a right to self-determination. Conformism is the attachment to a two-state solution as the only viable option for that right. I don't know how many states we might wrest from the future in what is now Israel and Palestine, or how many deaths stand between us and the arrival of that horizon of possibility. I am pretty sure, however, that most of the "futures past"—of two states, or Eretz Israel, or a return of all Palestinians to their original home or villages—are past indeed.

This resonates with how David Scott describes certain historical shifts as marked by an awareness that people develop, consciously or not, that "the prospect of old futures has faded from view and [has] unsettled, as a consequence, our prior notions about what to do with the pasts in the present."[133] In other words, if, before, we told a certain story about the past because that story was linked in some way to an imagined future, then the destruction of that possible future will change the stories we tell about the past as well.

There is a major debate emerging over the ways that legacy news outlets are covering the war. Many of the left have long criticized the mainstream media reports. Now, however, the complaints are coming from journalists themselves. Last week, protestors staged a sit-in in the lobby of the *New York Times*, claiming that it consistently favored Israel in its reporting of the Gaza war, and that it had, in effect, "laundered genocide."[134] Those who gathered were mostly journalists themselves, along with artists and other cultural workers.

Just two days ago, *Vanity Fair* printed a long report on the November 3 "resignation" of the award-winning *New York Times Magazine* writer Jazmine Hughes, a Black woman who had signed a letter (different from the one of November 9) protesting newsrooms' coverage of the Gaza war. Hughes was told by the *Times* editor that taking positions and going to protests is against *Times* policy (it is, but does not necessarily lead to losing your job). She resigned, she later said, "under pressure."[135]

Today, the *Washington Post* reported that Mona Chalabi of the *New York Times* had decided to make a statement to her editor just before she received the Pulitzer Prize for illustrated reporting. Sitting next to the Editor in Chief, Jake Silverstein, she leaned over to show him a chart she had just posted on Instagram, with data that showed how much more frequently the *Times* mentioned Israeli deaths than Palestinian ones.[136]

During any conflict, people on different sides will accuse media of bias: readers in a starkly partisan political and media landscape will complain when they read or see something that they disagree with. This is different. Journalists themselves are chafing against the limits they see being imposed—the guidelines not only about what they write in the paper, but what they post or even like on social media. There is a reason for mainstream news outlets to want their reporters to seem objective, with no documented political affiliations. And yet, in a social media world, this increasingly amounts to silencing some of our most articulate and knowledgeable commentators. Journalists want to report the world as they see it; they are increasingly unwilling to silently follow the company line.

NOVEMBER 19

The World Health Organization has declared Gaza's largest hospital, Al-Shifa, to be a "death zone," with only 25 staff left in place to care for 291 seriously ill patients. Al-Shifa is the site that Israel says has a Hamas command center underneath it, and it released video footage of a 55m tunnel underground.

There's been a huge amount of discussion about these tunnels: was there really a command center under the hospital? Are the reports of massive networks of tunnels true?

I find these questions rather useless. I assume that there are underground tunnels and command centers for a force of what was probably 30,000 fighters including both Hamas and Islamic Jihad. It does not change one bit the reality that it is simply immoral (and illegal) to bomb a hospital with people inside who cannot leave (or, because they are doctors caring for patients, will not). The bombs are not the only killers. At least 40 patients have died in the last week before they could evacuate, due to lack of electricity to operate equipment like dialysis machines and incubators.[137]

NOVEMBER 20

I sometimes imagine that one day historians will ask those of us alive today the same thing that Republican Senator Howard Baker asked about President Nixon in the Watergate hearings: "What did the president know and when did he know it?" They will look back at the Biden administration and the Netanyahu government and all the apologists for both, and they will ask if they really understood, early on, what they were doing to the world. They did. They do.

NOVEMBER 21

Today the IDF released the poet Mosab Abu Toha from detention after holding him for two days. Mosab is 31 years old, with a wife and three children. His first book in English, *Things You May Find Hidden in My Ear* (2022), won an American Book Award and was a finalist for the National Book Critics Circle Award.[138] He is the founder of the Edward Said library, with two branches in Gaza, holding the enclave's most significant collections of English books. On October 20, he had published an essay in the *New Yorker* about the early days of the war.[139]

Mosab was at home in Gaza City when the war began, when Israel dropped leaflets telling people in the city to leave their homes. Like many people, Mosab and his family were uncertain where to go; Gaza is densely populated and families are large. His uncle called to say that they could stay with the uncle's wife's family in the Jabalia camp, to the north of Gaza city. So they left, leaving behind the multi-generational family house, the lemon and olive trees, and Mosab's collection of books. His favorites include collections by Mahmoud Darwish and Naomi Shihab Nye, an Arab American who lives in Texas.

Arriving in Jabalia, they were soon without food. Israel had cut all access to food shipments, as well as electricity, water, fuel, and medicine. A week later, as Palestinians in the northern part of Gaza continued to move south, Mosab's family waited, as bombing seems incessant along the route to the south. Then, a couple of weeks ago, Mosab and his family got clearance to evacuate Gaza altogether. His son, just three years old, had been born when Mosab was studying in the US, and thus the boy was a US citizen. American officials have been trying to help American citizens and their families to evacuate at the Rafah checkpoint near Egypt. So, with his citizen son being cleared for evacuation, Mosab and his family found a man with a donkey and a cart and headed to the checkpoint.

The roads were crowded. Most people were walking, carrying children, along with what food and clothes they could. The lucky few had cars, or, like Mosab and his family, a donkey or a horse. Israeli soldiers lined the streets. Mosab was called out of the street by a soldier, told to leave his son and line up with some other men. He and around a dozen other men were commanded to undress in the street. You are Hamas, a soldier told him. "No! I've been in the US for the last four years," he replied. "I am not political." He was told to shut up. Some soldiers began kicking him, and they took him into custody. He was driven with others into southern Israel, interrogated for hours, beaten in the face and stomach.[140]

During this time, Mosab's friends in the US and elsewhere began mobilizing. Social media posts detailed what had happened, that he was in custody. He had spent a year at Harvard as a Scholar-at-Risk Fellow, and friends from Harvard were working to help. The *New Yorker* weighed in, tweeting about his detention, calling for his safe return. PEN International did the same.

Now, Mosab was one of the few Gazans that (some) American readers knew by name. A world of influential people were asking questions.

48 hours after being taken, Mosab was released. Shortly after, he and his family made it to the Egypt border crossing where the American passport worked its magic. He arrived safe in Cairo. Interviewed later, he still had no news of his parents, of his brother and his brother's wife, who was pregnant,

or of his sisters, each with three children. He felt certain that the Edward Said libraries were likely destroyed. He knew, too, that his home had been bombed, and, with it, all his books: the poetry collections and novels signed by American writers and friends.

He wanted to imagine a future. Grateful as he was for his family's safety, he was also devastated by his losses. "This future cannot be built on a land that is covered with blood and bones," he told *New Yorker* editor David Remnick in a podcast. In closing the interview, he asked Remnick to play his favorite song: "My Mother" by Marcel Khalife, with words by Mahmoud Darwish.[141]

NOVEMBER 22

As Thanksgiving approaches in the US, the Radcliffe Fellowship program puts up a board for Fellows to write what we are thankful for on post-it notes. Amidst the comments about "my family" and "good friends" someone writes: "The chance to be alive without being bombed every day."

In Khan Younis, they are beginning to make mass graves for all the bodies.[142]

NOVEMBER 23

Once in the early 2000s when I was teaching my undergraduate seminar on US-Middle East cultural encounters, I divided the students into two teams to "solve" the Israeli-Palestinian conflict. Many students at George Washington University hope to work in government or NGOs, so they like coming up with solutions rather than just asking hard questions. For decades, the mainstream conversation about how to solve the problem of Palestine had always revolved around Israeli security. How could Israel accept a

Palestinian state right next door when it was already surrounded by hostile Arab states? What kind of security guarantees could be offered when the territory of Israel was only nine miles wide at its narrowest point?

In this exercise, I asked each team (one Israel, one Palestine) to answer a few questions for their side. The first was: "What would it take for [Israel or Palestine] to feel secure?" The students didn't agree on what was needed, but they did all concur on one thing: it was the first time they had ever been asked to think about Palestinians as needing security too.

It will be different the next time I teach the course: there won't be any doubts about Palestinians as vulnerable to Israeli violence. The point of the exercise was really to have students think about what it would mean to consider Palestinians as fully equal in every way to Israelis—their lives equally as valuable, their rights equally deserving of protection.

The question was not only what Palestinians need to be secure. The question was why this had not been a question.

NOVEMBER 24

A couple of days ago, Israel's cabinet approved a deal that will allow the release of at least 50 hostages in exchange for about 150 Palestinians held in Israeli prisons. There will be a four-day ceasefire to facilitate the exchange. On each day of the ceasefire, a certain number will be released by each side. There are scenes of joy in Israel, as hostages, one only three years old, arrive home. Most are traumatized by their time in captivity. As they leave, a few of the hostages shake hands or hug their captors; this is shocking to the Israeli public, but some of the hostages insist that they were treated well. Almost 200 hostages remain in captivity.

There are similar scenes of celebration in Palestine, as the prisoners—almost all women and children—are released to their families. Some had been held in "administrative detention," a system that allows Israel to hold individuals without charge or trial or access to the allegations against them.

The resonances with another hostage story are striking. On November 4, 1979, a group of militant students in Iran took 65 Americans hostage in the US embassy. The Iranian revolution earlier that year had ousted the Shah of Iran, a brutal dictator and American ally, and placed an Islamic government in power, with Ayatollah Khomeini as the Supreme Leader. Now these militants had surprised everyone, seeming to put America in its place, showing its vulnerability when for so long it had functioned as the power behind the Shah's throne.

Six days after the takeover, ABC news began running a news special on the crisis every night at 11 p.m. Most people at ABC expected the special program to last two or three weeks until the crisis was resolved; instead *America Held Hostage* was on air every night for four months, until ABC replaced it with a more generic late-night news program, *Nightline*, anchored by Ted Koppel. Even then, the show highlighted the hostages frequently, and Koppel ended every show with a tally: "That's the news for March 10, the 128th day of the hostages' captivity."

ABC joined most other American television and news media in never letting the country forget the hostages, telling stories of their lives, their families. They became a symbol of America for Americans, not because they worked for the US embassy (and thus were "official Americans" in State Department lingo) but because they were presented as private individuals, as "typical Americans." This was a story of ordinary people caught up in "politics." Americans across the country tied yellow ribbons around trees or wore them on their sweaters to show their sympathy with the hostages.

For more than a year, the hostage families became a kind of affective icon in US life, interviewed frequently, with TV crews joining them at church services or family dinners. When there was an early release of several hostages, one young marine shocked the country when he told reports that he had learned a lot from his captors, and that he was "very saddened" about what the Shah had done when he was in power. He criticized how the US had supported the Shah's rule.[143] American commentators reacted with fury, or they explained his statement as a version of Stockholm syndrome. The hostages were supposed to be apolitical people, representing American innocence.

This is similar to how the hostages have been seen in Israel. Their posters are everywhere, and they represent one part of how Israel sees itself: a threatened yet buoyant people, just trying to live life, who want nothing more than to be left alone. Indeed, most of these hostages are not diplomats or officials, unlike those in Iran were. Some of the Gaza hostages have undoubtedly already been killed, either in the daily bombings or by their Hamas captors. Their victimization represents Israeli blamelessness, their endangerment highlights Israel's vulnerability. They have become icons, and icons can do richly layered cultural and political work for a nation at war.

NOVEMBER 28

The University of Pennsylvania denied a progressive Jewish group permission to show a 2023 documentary called *Israelism*, which shows how two different Jewish young people respond to their increasing awareness about Israel's treatment of Palestinians. Hunter College in New York had canceled the same film a week earlier. A few days after Penn's denial, the film went ahead as planned, with space secured by the school's Middle East Center. In response, the university threatened the students with disciplinary sanctions, and the director of the Middle East Center resigned.[144]

This doesn't come as a surprise. The right to pro-Palestinian speech is under attack across the country. Undoubtedly because we are seeing more of that speech, the backlash is now bigger and stronger than ever. It is astonishing to see how schools are backing down, and fast, from the principles of academic freedom and free speech. Faculty and especially students are being sanctioned for offering opinions, even outside of the classroom.

The legal situation is different for public and private universities. Public universities are required to uphold the same free speech rights that people have as citizens; they are operating in state-owned space and so are (theoretically) less able to police student or faculty conduct that is otherwise legal. Private universities have choices in the matter: Christian schools can require Christian beliefs and prevent the distribution of flyers about atheism, for example. But most major private universities have agreed to protect both academic freedom (for faculty, in terms of their research and writing) and free speech (which applies to both students and faculty). Most universities have codes of conduct that prevent intimidation or harassment; those might be more tightly drawn than public laws are. In general, the assumption has been that individuals can say unpopular things in university settings, and, as long as they are not targeting other individuals or making a threat, the university will support their right to speech.

And yet. Films are being canceled. Donors are making calls. Senators are making speeches. Activist student groups have been suspended at several schools. The Middle East Studies Association's Committee on Academic Freedom has been busier than I've ever seen it. The Committee investigates allegations of violations of the academic freedom or free speech rights of students or professors and writes letters of protest to high-level administrators and sometimes Board members in academic institutions. Their letters span an array of issues. Since October, one faculty member was asked to take two readings on Israel-Palestine off her Critical Race Theory syllabus. Two teaching assistants were fired at UT Austin for sending an email to students saying that they understood some students were experiencing "mental health implications" from the war and that they did not support the university's silence on the issue. My own school, George Washington University, suspended Students for Justice in Palestine for projecting pro-Palestinian slogans onto the university library. These events are different but share the same messaging: administrators around the country will punish both faculty and students for speaking in particular ways about the war.[145]

It makes me think about the ramifications if I were to be teaching my US-Middle East Cultural Encounters class. I would be naive not to be a bit nervous. In my US in the World class, I can spend the semester talking about US empire with little controversy. Students might be upset by what they learn about US-backed coups or the conduct of the Iraq war; they may even angrily disagree with parts of my lectures. But they don't report me for "anti-Americanism."

NOVEMBER 29

Today is officially the International Day of Solidarity with Palestine. Not much seems to be happening in the way of demos, but my WhatsApp group of pro-Palestinian Radcliffe Fellows is alive with messages about the film cancelations, various protests, the hostage-prisoner exchanges. It's a diverse group, who are clear in their positions and generally furious about what is happening to Palestinians and their supporters. "Standing in solidarity" would be exactly the way to describe them.

But what is solidarity, exactly? The expectation or longing for solidarity is a cry for justice against a universe determinedly insensitive to our demands. When we think of solidarity, maybe we think of a line of people, arm-in-arm, facing down the police. Or a woman's refusal to cross a picket line at the factory gates.

Or the Black Power fists of Tommie Smith and John Carlos at the 1968 Olympics. Or something as simple and brave as young Rachel Corrie standing in front of an Israeli bulldozer that was destroying Palestinian homes—and paying with her life.[146] All of these are impassioned visions, offering a performance of moral clarity and a willingness to take a stand.

Solidarity is more than an ideological or intellectual statement; it is infused with feeling. Drawing on scholar Sara Ahmed, I think of solidarity as being as much an emotion as an action. For Ahmed, emotions do not work in the way we often think. Emotions like love or anger, she says, do not start from inside the person and move outward. Nor do they start from the outside and move in, as we might picture the emotions that emerge at a concert or in a crowd. Instead, Ahmed argues, emotions circulate, through a sense that people share. We are impressed upon by a situation, a person, or an object, and in the wake of that, we turn toward or away from it.[147] Ahmed (and a whole range of other scholars) often use the term "affect" to distinguish the way they think about the public nature of feeling, and the importance of emotion to ideology: how it helps ideas connect, makes them seem right. "Affect is what sticks," Ahmed says, "or what sustains or preserves the connection between ideas, values, and objects."[148] Solidarity is an affective thing because it connects our feelings and our beliefs with the worlds we endure as well as the ones we hope to make.

There was a time in the 1960s and 1970s when "Third World solidarity" was a mantra, a talisman, and sometimes a truth. Palestinians and African Americans met in North African capitals; Cubans and Angolans fought side-by-side; American antiwar protestors chanted the name of Ho Chi Minh.[149] These are not all equivalent, but they required a particular kind of moral geography, a vision of "three worlds" that was beyond what could be plotted on a map—a matter of political commitment or affective attachment.

Some historians have seen that Third World solidarity as epitomized in the 1955 Bandung Conference, officially the Asian-African Conference. At that meeting, African American observers joined with luminaries of the decolonizing world, including Nasser of Egypt, Sukarno of Indonesia, and Nehru of India—three leaders who seemed to represent the possibilities of independence. The retrospective myth of Bandung is that it was the moment when "the darker peoples" of the world chose solidarity with each other and against the imperialist powers.[150]

Today, not surprisingly, historians have revisited and revisioned the heroic version of Bandung. The conference mattered because it made clear that colonialism was entering its endgame. Nonetheless, tensions among the intellectuals and political leaders of the emerging Third World were everywhere. By the early 1960s, there were competing visions (Asian-African solidarity versus a more global non-alignment, for example), and competition for leadership (e.g. Nasser v. Nehru; Nasser v. Kwame Nkrumah). A decade after Bandung, there would be competing conferences, a multitude of alliances, and as many schisms.[151]

The revisionist histories are crucial, then, because there is something in the popular storytelling about that moment—the way we narrate anti-colonial solidarity as a kind of swelling rise of unity-in-diversity, with Africans and Asians and Arabs all joining together, frictionless, through the symbols of the clenched fist or the Palestinian keffiyeh. The reality, we know, was different, more complex and much more underwritten by power politics within and between states, amongst different groups of Marxists or Black nationalists or liberals. There is a way in which even the term "solidarity" demands no cracks, no wavering in its solid-ness. That in turn can undercut the *work* of it, the failures, the realpolitik of making a stand. If we expect the promise of solidarity as energizing and seamless, will we find coalition and struggle to be unacceptably workmanlike?

This has nagged at me since my activist days, when Mobilization for Survival was quite clear that we were *not* solidarity activists. We didn't necessarily agree with everything the PLO did, or the ANC in South Africa, or the FMLN in El Salvador. We understood that we had a particular task as Americans, and our focus was on changing US policy. We had a vision of justice, and we recognized that our agendas, our policy statements, our hopes for peace, might be somewhat different than the agendas of people where US policy was doing harm. We would oppose US aid to El Salvador's brutal military dictatorship, but that did not mean we supported the revolutionary FMLN that was trying to take power. (Some of us did, some did not.) We didn't provide material support to the African National Congress (ANC), but we did fight for US sanctions on apartheid South Africa. It was an awkward dance. Some in my political community found it pretty damned wishy washy.

Yet I still stand somewhere in that space: I cannot be in solidarity with Hamas, or the PLO. But I can stand in solidarity with the idea of a free Palestine, firm in my conviction that a Palestinian freedom will make for a better world—one with one less devastating injustice, where we affirm that ordinary people can work with and for each other, across borders, to make a difference.

Scholars Atalia Omer and Joshua Lupo write that solidarities often break apart: individual activists are sometimes "unable to participate in an intersectional vision of emancipation that transcends national boundaries."[152] We are all shaped by hegemonic frameworks of state powers, racial hegemonies, religious divides, and dominant ideologies. If solidarity is our designated object—the desired good around which so many political projects have oriented—then disappointed hope is its first-born. Back in the '80s, the self-aware feminist letter ended not with "in solidarity," but with "yours in struggle."[153] It wasn't supposed to be easy.

Solidarity is never solid. If we could paint it, it would be striated and seamed, remarkably aged and ragged, but with bits of hopeful new growth—winding wildly in spirals or staggering in one direction only to switch sharply to another. Perhaps solidarity grows *only* in the soil of struggle. That soil forms each of us who commits. We come with our own agendas but also an ability to listen and learn; we struggle together to cultivate new possibilities out of difficulty and sweat and determination.

DECEMBER 3

Today we learned that Hisham Awartani is paralyzed from the chest down. Awartani was one of three young Palestinian men who were attacked in Vermont late last month. The three friends were walking up the street in Middlebury, all wearing keffiyehs, when a 48-year-old white man stepped out of his front door and shot them. The other two young men are stable. All three had grown up in the West Bank and had come to the US for college.

Awartani is a student at Brown University. Earlier this week students there gathered for a vigil. Professor Beshara Doumani read a message from Hisham: "As much as I appreciate the love [of] every single one of you here today, I am but one casualty in a much wider conflict [...] This is why when you say your wishes and light your candles for me today, your mind should not just be focused on me as an individual, but rather as a proud member of a people being oppressed."[154]

DECEMBER 5

Efforts to extend the truce with Hamas fell apart a few days ago, and heavy fighting broke out across the Gaza strip. Israel's defense minister explains that "Hamas only understands force and therefore we will continue to act until we achieve the goals of war."[155] Yesterday Israel announced that Gazans should evacuate Khan Younis, where many of them fled after the first evacuation. It is utterly unclear where they should go—there is no safe space. Gaza is being flattened, people are hungry and ill, homeless and crowded beyond measure. The WHO had already announced that illness was likely to kill more Palestinians than bombs.

Reuters runs the headline: "Israel orders Gazans to flee, bombs where it sends them."[156] You can't make this stuff up.

Three college presidents, all women, testify before Congress on issues of antisemitism on campus. Claudine Gay from Harvard, Liz Magill of the University of Pennsylvania, and Sally Kornbluth of MIT were harangued by members of the House Education and Workforce Committee. These academic leaders said many things right, condemning antisemitism and saying that they wanted to make sure their communities understood and recognized its seriousness. Magill defended her decision to allow a Palestinian literature festival at Penn to go forward in September, stating: "Canceling that event would have been inconsistent with academic freedom and free expression."

The congressional committee, angered by pro-Palestinian demonstrations on campuses, demanded whether students had been expelled or faculty members disciplined for making remarks the representatives deemed antisemitic. They made no distinction between criticism of Israel and harassment or attacks on Jewish students. They defined the term "Intifada" (which literally means "uprising" or "shaking off") as a call to kill Jews. Magill was then shown a video of a student protest with chants of "globalize the Intifada." I'm not sure what Magill thought "Intifada" meant, but she didn't challenge the just-plain-wrong definition offered by the committee. Instead, she immediately responded that the video was "very hard to watch." She understood why many people would be afraid seeing such chanting. "I believe at a minimum it is hate speech and should be condemned." [157]

This makes me furious, but I admit I feel bad for all three of these presidents. In the first place, this has been a hellish time to try to guide a university, and Harvard's Gay, at least, is brand new in the job. Second, they are not really there for a hearing on academic freedom or antisemitism. They are there so a group of Republicans can yell at them for having commitment to Diversity, Equity, and Inclusion. New hiring (and perhaps admissions) practices, the interrogators imply, are leading to an increase in hatred of Jewish people. (Read: all these Black, Latinx, Asian, and Arab professors are teaching their students to hate Jews.) This isn't just about this war or this conflict: several scholars have documented the decades-long impact of right-wing billionaires to try to reshape American education and weed out liberalism.[158]

Both McGill and Gay were asked a no-win question of whether calling for the genocide of Jews is protected speech. (There were no members of either of their universities calling for any such thing.) Isn't calling for genocide by definition bullying or harassment, the congressional representatives asked? And both presidents said it would depend on context: whether it was targeted at an individual, whether it was linked to student conduct, etc. The university could condemn that speech, but they might not necessarily punish the speaker if what that person said was protected speech. Each of them had been eloquent about how important they deemed the fight against antisemitism in campus and in classrooms, but both could have done a better job in making clear that the university could speak out strongly against certain speech and try to improve campus climates in ways other than disciplining students or professors for unpopular opinions. In the eyes of a number of important people, however, neither president did what they were supposed to do: promise these Senators that their university would punish those whose speech was deemed unacceptable.[159]

DECEMBER 7

Two contemporary Palestinian poets, two different fates. Like Mosab Abu Toha, Refaat Alareer was in Gaza as the war began. At 44 years old, with six children, he was killed yesterday by an IDF airstrike along with six members of his family: his brother, sister, and four of his nieces and nephews.[160] Alareer taught English literature at the Islamic University of Gaza, where he was known for encouraging students to create. He was the editor of two short story collections: *Gaza Writes Back: Short Stories from Young Writers in Gaza, Palestine* (2013) and *Gaza Unsilenced* (2015).[161]

"Let it be a story" was Alareer's motto; he believed deeply in the power of narration to change a world.[162] In May of 2021, Alareer had written a guest essay in the *New York Times* as Israel was attacking Gaza in a flare-up of the ongoing conflict with Hamas. The essay was less about the attack per se than about his family's attempt to celebrate his six-year-old daughter's birthday despite the near-constant missile bombardments. He was writing, in essence, about how to continue to live life in the face of the horrors of the intermittent wars: how to find some chocolate biscuits for a little girl, when a cake was impossible.[163]

Two years later, Alareer was dead. Anticipating this real possibility, he had pinned a poem, "If I Must Die," to the top of his Twitter feed:

If I must die,
you must live
to tell my story
to sell my things
to buy a piece of cloth
and some strings,
(make it white with a long tail)
so that a child, somewhere in Gaza
while looking heaven in the eye
awaiting his dad who left in a blaze —
and bid no one farewell
not even to his flesh
not even to himself —
sees the kite, my kite you made, flying up above,

and thinks for a moment an angel is there
bringing back love.
If I must die
let it bring hope,
let it be a story.[164]

We all need to know more stories of Palestine, of all types. Alareer surely would have been pleased to know that his poem soon was everywhere on the internet, with celebrities and people on TikTok from all over the world filming themselves reading it aloud. It was ubiquitous, even if only for a moment.

But now I'm thinking back to a rather different poem by Noor Hindi from 2020, titled "Fuck Your Lecture on Craft, My People are Dying." It's a meditation on what "beauty" possibly means in a time of such ongoing destruction:

Colonizers write about flowers.
I tell you about children throwing rocks at Israeli tanks
seconds before becoming daisies.

Hindi goes on to describe what occupation does to poetry. And she ends her piece in a way that is both reminiscent of Alareer's poem and utterly distinct from its sensibility:

When I die, I promise to haunt you forever.
One day, I'll write about the flowers like we own them.[165]

DECEMBER 8

The UN Secretary-General, António Guterres, once again urges the Security Council to support a ceasefire in Gaza. Guterres has been suggesting, requesting, calling for, essentially begging for a ceasefire since October 19. Now he takes a stronger step, invoking Article 99, which allows him to put an item on the Security Council's agenda. (This is the first time in 50 years a Secretary-General has invoked Article 99, which highlights the seriousness of the issue while also perhaps saying something about the hidebound nature of UN protocol.) "The people of Gaza are being told to move like human pinballs—ricocheting between ever-smaller slivers of the south, without any of the basics for survival—but nowhere in Gaza is safe," Guterres told the Security Council.[166] To the surprise of no one, the US vetoed the resolution.

DECEMBER 9

36 years ago today something extraordinary happened in Palestine. The people in the West Bank and Gaza rose up in a series of demonstrations and acts of civil disobedience that became known as the Intifada. (Later, there would be a Second Intifada, and this 1980s movement would retroactively come to be called the First Intifada.) The Intifada was indeed a "shaking off": people on the ground in the Occupied Territories began to resist the occupation in new and remarkable ways.

The Intifada was not started or coordinated by the PLO. In fact, some people viewed it as the local Palestinians on the ground in the Occupied Territories wresting back power from the PLO leadership, which had left Beirut in 1982 and landed mostly in far-off Tunis. In the Palestinian camps and towns, residents developed a mélange of resistance measures: strikes, graffiti, boycotts, and blocking roads the Israeli military used to rule the territories. Partly the actions came in response to Defense Minister Yitzhak Rabin's "Iron Fist" policy, put in place in 1985 as a strategy for meeting all Palestinian active resistance with overwhelming force. One could argue that the Iron Fist not only helped instigate the Intifada, it was also what made it work. Putting up a Palestinian flag could get you arrested. Planning a strike or painting graffiti were illegal. The absurdity of Israel's level of policing could be made apparent by simply hoisting a Palestinian flag with foreign media in the vicinity, as tanks and police cars arrived to haul off a young person to prison. The classic image from those times is children throwing stones at Israeli tanks—a perfect David versus Goliath set piece.

Eventually a unified coordinating group emerged, which would issue dates for strikes or call for protests. But each village and refugee camp also operated somewhat on its own, with women in particular taking unprecedented leadership roles.[167] It was a new, younger generation, raised within Palestine, taking back the initiative from the organized PLO and forging their own visions of how to fight for freedom. In the United States, it was a powerful and empowering time, because people were seeing Palestinians differently. The Israeli invasion of 1982 had led to changed views of Israelis, but it was only in 1987–88 that many media outlets began, hesitatingly, to represent Palestinians in richer, more sympathetic ways—to tell their stories not only as either terrorists or (occasional) abject victims, but as activists and organizers, people working through local democratic practices to change the long game of the Israeli occupation of the West Bank and Gaza, then in its twentieth year.[168]

I traveled to the West Bank with other American activists in 1988. We had arranged a sister city project between Cambridge, MA, and Ramallah. While there, we met with groups of local organizers; women running childcare and healthcare facilities that Israel was not providing; groups planning regular marches and staging dramatic confrontations. We saw, too, the injuries sustained by people shot with rubber bullets. This could happen in retaliation when stones were thrown at tanks, but activists also threw stones and sometimes Molotov cocktails at cars and buses carrying settlers. They wanted the settlers to feel their fury, to feel unsafe traveling back to homes that had been built on Palestinian land.

Mostly, though, the First Intifada was a mass uprising based on civil disobedience, one that seemed for a while as if it might lead to a genuine Palestinian state.[169] The PLO saw this as an opportunity to both mobilize the attention of the world and to state clearly that it renounced all violence. In December of 1988, the US opened negotiations with the PLO for the first time.

The Second Intifada, which began in 2000 (after Oslo had clearly failed to deliver what it promised), was a different thing: more violent, and less hopeful. Palestinian suicide bombings had been relatively rare before, but now the numbers rose starkly, with many carried out in city centers. Between 2000 and 2005, there were 138 suicide attacks, which killed 657 people and injured 3,682.[170] I assume that is why some people today think they can retroactively claim that the word itself means "kill Jews."[171] They are wrong. The Second Intifada embodied hopelessness and fury, but it never meant genocide.

For many people who lived through the late 1980s, "Intifada" means just the opposite of genocide or violence: it was grassroots activism, self-organized civil disobedience, and a willingness to suffer bullets and imprisonment for the sake of a cause. It was a liberation moment, decentralized and led from below, that finally had the media's attention.

Tonight I watched a video of an outdoor reading of one of Refaat Alareer's poems at a vigil in New York. The poem, read by a young Black woman, was "I Am You." Addressing himself to an Israeli soldier, Alareer makes a set of connections between Jewish suffering and Palestinian suffering. The young woman read it beautifully. What is really striking in the video is the young and diverse crowd watching. Once again there is a mix of Black and Brown and Asian and white people. A few wear keffiyehs. One woman holds up a sign: "If you ever lose hope, remember this crowd."[172]

DECEMBER 10

My own history as an activist in the 1980s has sometimes made me cautious, perhaps overly so. When some of my friends first started organizing for Boycott, Divestment, and Sanctions against Israel more than a decade ago, I argued quietly against the Boycott part. Divestment made sense: a non-violent campaign that would allow us to target US corporations as well as Israeli ones, such as the campaign against Caterpillar for providing equipment that Israel uses to destroy Palestinian homes.

Sanctions seemed a long way off, but at least that focused us on what the US does: asking to end US support for Israeli settlements or to stop sending weapons used against Palestinians.

Boycott seemed more contentious. Ok, if that meant refusing to buy products made in the settlements or from enterprises whose owners opposed Palestinian rights; we can get sandals and soda-making machines elsewhere. But not going to academic conferences in Israel; not inviting Israeli speakers or musicians or academics to the US? I knew how bad that might look. The ban was supposed to focus only on institutions, not individuals, but it was messy in practice, especially in the first few years.[173]

It had been easy with South Africa, since the boycott mostly affected white South Africans. In fact, it was brilliant. The South Africa boycott was most active and successful around sports; it began when South Africa's all-white teams were banned from the Olympics starting in 1964. Slowly, they were forbidden in other sports: tennis and soccer and then, closest to home, rugby. Those segregated teams were perfect emblems of the apartheid system, and the boycott strategies were some of the most energizing and visible for organizers.

Boycotting Israel carried a different kind of weight, even as a form of non-violent and symbolic resistance, in part because Israel had and still has a far deeper well of support in the US than white South Africa ever did. I feared the boycott would hurt the movement more than it would help, that we would end up talking more about the potential suffering of Israeli academics than the actual suffering of Palestinian academics—and doctors, and children, and bus drivers—who were living under daily oppression.

Maybe I was right. The boycott certainly did cause tremendous backlash. The American Studies Association, for example, voted to support a boycott of Israeli academic institutions in December 2013. The group was immediately faced with a great deal of negative press.[174] Soon 80 university presidents joined to condemn the organization.[175] There were the ongoing lawsuits, and over the next decade, the ASA spent a great deal of money and energy defending itself in court over what was essentially a symbolic action.

But I was also wrong. Because, in the end, the BDS movement has done more to raise awareness about Palestine than anything else in a very long time. It has given people a political focus and a concrete sense of what they can do. Since the ASA's vote, scores of academic institutions have voted to support some form of boycott. Those, too, are symbolic votes, in that they do not have significant material impact.

But the symbolism is precisely what matters. To say that Israel should be subject to sanctions and boycott is to say that what is happening to Palestinians is so immoral that it requires rituals of disengagement from the perpetrator. No wonder the BDS movement has been treated by Israel and its supporters as an existential threat. It questions the foundations of Israel's story about its own inherent righteousness.

DECEMBER 11

I'm reading more and more of Darwish, and now I have picked up his *Memory for Forgetfulness: August, Beirut, 1982*. This memoir recounts his activities on August 6,

1982, the deadliest day of bombardment during Israel's siege of Beirut.[176] (It was also, as Darwish notes, the anniversary of the US nuclear bombing of Hiroshima in 1945.) Darwish was living in Lebanon then; he had left Israel in 1969, moved to Cairo briefly, and had then joined the Palestine Research Center in Beirut, an arm of the PLO.

If we think of how our sense of time moves forward and backward, how the changes in the horizon of possibility of any given moment shape our understanding of what has come before, then it makes sense to me that this world-tilting devastation in Gaza might return us anew to the 1982 invasion. At that moment, too, Israel also aimed to destroy a major source of Palestinian resistance.

When Israel began its siege of Beirut in June of 1982, the immediate catalyst was the attempt by the extremist Palestinian faction, the Abu Nidal Organization, to assassinate the Israeli ambassador to the United Kingdom. The underlying goal was something else: Israel was tired of having the PLO headquartered on its northern border; there had been attacks back and forth for years. Many of the Palestinians who had been displaced from their homes in 1948 and in 1967 had fled to Lebanon; as many as 300,000 people had settled in the country's south. The poorest of those went to refugee camps set up by the United Nations. The Lebanese government had been less than enthusiastic about this refugee flow; they soon established laws that prevented Palestinians from owning property, from working in various jobs, or from becoming Lebanese citizens. Starting in 1969, an agreement between the Lebanese government and the PLO put governing the refugee camps into the hands of the PLO.

When Israel launched its invasion in June of 1982, it wanted to end Palestinian rocket attacks and infiltration into northern Israel. In 1978, for example, Fatah had hijacked a bus and killed dozens of Israelis. The attacks went both ways; Israel had shelled the Palestinian camps and southern Lebanese villages repeatedly. But Israel's goals were larger; it not only wanted to end the border hostilities, it wanted to get rid of the PLO altogether, by destroying it or forcing it to relocate. That, Israeli leaders believed, might also destroy or at least seriously weaken Palestinian nationalism in the occupied territories of the West Bank and Gaza.

That summer, Israel's military rolled through the Palestinian camp in the south and continued all the way to Beirut, which it besieged for two months. Darwish's meditation on the siege, written six years later, is intimate. The poet describes his fear as he walks down the streets that are being shelled—not only a fear of death, but of dying alone. "I am terrified of falling among the ruins, prey to a moaning no one can hear."[177]

As he recounts the day, interweaving it with Arab history and political commentary, Darwish also notes his own mood swings and confusion. The rockets are landing in the city. "Yet I want to break into song. Yes, I want to sing to this burning day. I do want to sing. I want to find a language that transforms language itself into steel for the spirit—a language to use against these sparkling silver insects, these jets."[178]

He writes powerfully of the young Palestinians from the refugee camps who are fighting the Israeli invasion. These youth have never known Palestine, have only heard about it in stories. Darwish observes they have "also read a great deal in the books of their bodies and their shacks."[179] Their current lives as refugees tell their own stories about worlds destroyed and lost.

Some of the most powerful moments in the book are Darwish's attention to the small pleasures and beauties, his insistence on listening to birds and noticing the changing light. He waxes eloquent on the importance of coffee, its aroma, its healing powers: "I need five minutes. I want a five-minute truce for the sake of coffee."

The book ends with a dream, and perhaps a death. The narrator has moved into despair; he is far from the wine and rainbows he once saw in Palestine's future. The sea is overcoming him. The sea drops from the sky, enters his room. "I don't want the sea," he says.

I see nothing in the sea except the sea.
I don't see a shore.
I don't see a dove.[180]

Israel withdrew from West Beirut after the PLO agreed to move to Tunis in late August of 1982. Darwish went with them. The Israeli military maintained its presence in southern Lebanon, however, trying to wipe out what was left of Palestinian resistance. It was confronted with people who were fighting for their homes, and the war became a long, difficult slog. Israel killed at least 5,000 civilians in Beirut, and many thousands of others as it razed refugee camps in the south. Over the course of the war and the ensuing 18-year occupation, approximately 50,000 people were killed or injured in Lebanon.

DECEMBER 12

There are a lot of people talking about Israel's actions as genocide. They suggest the goal is to make Gaza uninhabitable, or simply to kill as many Gazans as possible in a fury of retaliation for October 7. Some right-wing politicians have acknowledged as much. Galit Distel-Atbaryan, Israel's former Minister of Information, called for Israel to erase "all of Gaza from the face of the earth" and drive its residents into Egypt.[181]

Genocide is a legal designation, and despite the vicious rhetoric from Israel's right, I'm not totally sure that is what we are seeing. Still, the word choice is of secondary significance.

Gaza is being systematically destroyed, and the attacks on civilians are too frequent, too consistent, to be anything other than, at best, a wanton and willful disregard for civilian life carried out under the aegis of rooting out Hamas. According to political analyst Daniel Levy and journalist Tony Karon, Israel's actions suggest that the goal is "to push for expulsion via a militarily engineered humanitarian catastrophe."[182]

What is unclear is whether Israel has any kind of coherent plan, any cogent sense of where they or Gaza will be after this relentless war. Sometimes it seems like the idea is to herd Palestinians to the border and pressure Egypt to take them into the Sinai. Or perhaps the aim is to contain Gazans even more tightly into the south of this already tiny space, which will then be ever more tightly governed by Israel.

Israeli officials are also declaring openly that the two-state solution is "off the table." The Likud government has never accepted the idea of a real Palestinian state, but now the death of Oslo is official. Israel's ambassador to the United Kingdom told a stunned interviewer for Sky Media that Israel was looking to new frameworks. Asked if those frameworks would include a Palestinian state, he said "Absolutely no."[183]

DECEMBER 13

The hopes of the families of Israeli hostages are waning. There has been less mention of them in the US media, and, from what I can tell, the same is true in Israel. With the bombardment of Gaza, many of the 138 who are left are surely dead now. There seems to be no move toward another ceasefire or exchange. Israel is pumping seawater into the underground tunnels where Hamas was holding some hostages. In a meeting between family members and Netanyahu, the Prime Minister was barely sympathetic; he all but said directly that he had gotten out all the hostages he could.[184]

The press has also begun to report that some of the people who died in the initial Hamas attack were killed by Israeli forces. There are reports of Israeli soldiers shooting in confusion at the music festival, aiming at the guerillas but accidentally hitting some festivalgoers. Other reports indicate that in the Be'eri kibbutz, a general ordered soldiers to fire shells into a house where he knew there were still hostages.[185] Eventually, there will surely be some kind of reckoning with this in Israel.

DECEMBER 14

CNN's Clarissa Ward goes into Gaza for the first time. This is remarkable in itself; almost no US-based reporter has been in Gaza once since the beginning of the war. Ward explains that Israel and Egypt have made it next-to-impossible for foreign journalists to get into the Strip. The tone of her report is striking: it is both sympathetic and hard-hitting. CNN's overall reporting has been pretty awful up to this point—distinctly oriented toward repeating Israel's talking points.[186]

But today, CNN's seven-minute story—a long report for TV—begins with Ward pointing out that Israel has hit Gaza with more than 22,000 strikes. "That, by far, surpasses anything we've seen in modern warfare," she says, as her vehicle travels along a road surrounded by bombed-out buildings and rubble. She meets a doctor at the Emirati Field Hospital, interviewing him with the sounds of bombs nearby. The most compelling moment is when Ward speaks with a little girl in the hospital. Ward speaks enough Arabic to do her own interview, and as she talks to the injured girl and her mother, tears flow down her cheeks. I've been watching mainstream coverage of the Middle East for 40 years, and I've never seen anything quite like it.[187] Perhaps the mainstream broadcasters have figured out that news is getting out via Palestinian journalists and they can no longer just continue to report the news of officialdom.

DECEMBER 15

As I write this notebook, I keep returning to the question of how to put together so many layered events, past and present, especially given how multiple conflicts in the Middle East often refract and repeat each other. The ongoing US "Global War on Terror" has led to so many military encounters, by America or its allies, which somehow seem to switch out locations and enemies without ever changing the script of street battles and improvised explosives and civilian dead. Even focusing just on Gaza is weirdly repetitive. Which Gaza war are we talking about again? Is it the 2023 one, or the smaller one in 2021, or maybe 2014, or 2008? I wonder if, in a few hundred years, there will be archeologists who excavate Gaza, carefully giving dates to each layer of missile remnants and building rubble? Or will it simply be known as "the long Gaza war"? Perhaps they will not remember it all. Most likely, much of Gaza will have long disappeared in the rising seas of environmental catastrophe.

DECEMBER 18

A group of faculty from across the country have sent out a petition to oppose what they call the "repressive climate on campuses." They single out an event at Syracuse University (NY), where a group of students who were holding a peaceful "study-in" for Palestine were threatened with academic sanctions for carrying signs that included the word "Intifada." This word, administrators said, "has been deemed by [Syracuse University] to be threatening," adding that it can be "reasonably interpreted" as a "call to the genocide of Jewish people." The faculty letter insisted that such an interpretation was not at all reasonable. It pointed out that this kind of action was taking place within a national climate in which pro-Palestinian groups were being suspended at several universities for non-violent protests, events on the war are abruptly canceled, and university administrators are suddenly creating new policies that require more administrative approval for student events. I tried to sign the letter, but they shut down accepting signatures before I could. More than 600 faculty from across the country had already added their names.[188]

DECEMBER 19

Ibrahim Musa, 27 year-old member of one of Gaza's civil defense teams, tells a reporter: "I cannot sleep, not even for one minute. I am constantly haunted by the voices and screams of people under the rubble as they beg us to pull them out."[189]

DECEMBER 20

My friend and Radcliffe colleague Joelle Abi-Rached publishes a piece in the *Boston Review* on the "war on hospitals." She's an historian of medicine and an MD—the same person I was texting with in the early days of the war. Her essay pulls together some of the horrific statistics of hospitals bombed and healthcare workers killed (283 in Gaza so far). I find her most powerful argument is about the silence of the US medical establishment.

The American Medical Association, for example, had put out a strong statement condemning the Russian attacks on Ukraine, saying that "the AMA is outraged by the senseless injury and death the Russian army has inflicted on the

Ukrainian people." Its statement on Gaza, on the other hand, is remarkably muted, saying the organization "supports efforts to deliver humanitarian aid and medical supplies to those facing a humanitarian crisis." There are no actors here, no Israeli invasion or bombing, and the identity of "those" facing crisis remains unsaid.

Joelle's essay lists the numerous attacks on hospitals. Not only the bombing of Al-Shifa, Gaza's largest, but also the forced evacuation of Al-Rantisi Specialized Hospital for Children, the destruction of a nearby pediatric hospital, and that of the International Eye Hospital. The Turkish-Palestinian hospital ran out of fuel and could no longer function; the Indonesian hospital was targeted by a missile and lost all electricity; it is no longer in service. There remains only one functioning hospital in the north of Gaza strip.[190]

The piece is scientific, scholarly, and calm. Joelle herself, on the other hand, is outraged all the time. On our WhatsApp group, she sends out links to interviews, quotes from Arab or Greek philosophers, a bit of French existential literature—all commentary on the absurdity of the world we find ourselves in. I admire her unflagging energy, her ability to remain appalled but not cynical, even when she is not surprised in the slightest by each day's horrors.

DECEMBER 21

Israel is a "Jewish state," which means, according to its own logic, that it cannot be Israel if it is not dominated (numerically, culturally) by Jews. The journalist Ezra Klein made an argument on his podcast yesterday that the idea of a Jewish state is not a particular moral problem, even though some non-Zionists or anti-Zionists argue that it is inherently discriminatory. Every state is similar, Klein said, in the sense that "a state is for the people who it has defined itself as being for. America is a state for Americans, China for the Chinese, Brazil for the Brazilians."[191] And if a person doesn't fit that state's definition of who it is for, that person can't just show up and have citizenship. So, on this point, Klein insists, Israel is not that unusual.

There are a number of problems with this argument. First, Israel defines itself as a state for Jews everywhere, and not only a state for those (including some Palestinians) who are its citizens. It is an ethnic state with a global vision. Second, Israeli law is designed to limit the space that Palestinians citizens of the state can occupy. It is very difficult for Palestinians to buy land, either in Israel or in the Palestinian territories. According to Human Rights Watch, Israeli policy "restricts Palestinians to dense population centers while maximizing the land available for Jewish communities."[192] Finally, even if it were correct that Israel defines its citizens the way, say, the United States did for most of its history, then that too would be a problem. The historical parallels are not flattering. Just as Israel limits both immigration and citizenship to maintain a large Jewish majority, the United States did something quite similar. Before the middle of the twentieth century, the US had national immigration quotas designed to keep out all non-white people and even some Europeans, especially Jews and Italians.

In addition, the definition of who could become a naturalized US citizen was explicitly limited by race from the 1790 Naturalization Act until the Immigration and Nationality Act of 1952 (the McCarran-Walter Act). During that 162-year period, only "free white persons" could become naturalized citizens. The Fourteenth Amendment in 1868 provided for the citizenship of former slaves, but both before and after that one-time exemption, the United States officially defined itself as a country that offered only "white" immigrants a path to citizenship. Figuring out who was or was not white (Syrians? South Asians? Mexicans?) was the source of a vigorous and contradictory set of judicial rulings in the nineteenth and early twentieth centuries. In that sense, the United States was a nation "for" white people, even though other people lived in its borders, with some (but not equal) rights.[193]

That is no longer the case, legally. The US eliminated the racial barrier to naturalization in 1952 and eliminated national quotas on immigration in 1965. (There are still broad immigration limits on the number of individuals who can immigrate from the Western hemisphere and a separate, equally expansive cap for the Eastern Hemisphere.) The net result of the 1965 Hart-Celler Immigration Act was to transform dramatically the demographics of the US population. In 1960, 84% of US immigrants were born in Europe or Canada; in 2017, it was 13%.[194] Our country is far more Latinx, more Asian, and noticeably more of African and Middle Eastern origin than it once was, precisely because the state redefined who it was "for".

Of course, the visa and immigration system is notoriously hellish, especially since 9/11. And it was only in 1964 and 1965 that the Civil Rights Act and Voting Rights Act gave African Americans full legal rights and protection. Racism of all sorts remains a defining, often deadly, feature of our society. Nonetheless, what all of that history means is that, in the US today, unlike in Israel, there is no legal bar by ethnicity, religion, or race in terms of immigration, naturalization, voting, or property owning.

There are plenty of people who would turn back the clock. The white backlash against the inevitability of losing white numerical and cultural dominance has been profound. Thus President Trump's campaign promise of a giant border wall to keep out Mexicans and Central Americans, and his multiple attempts at promulgating a "Muslim ban" in 2017. The Trump administration saw two versions of his executive order restricting immigration from certain Muslim majority nations struck down by the courts, but in June 2018, the Supreme Court upheld a third version. The administration went on to expand the order to include nationals from 13 different countries before the ban was revoked by President Biden on his first day in office in 2021.[195]

So Klein is right; Israel is not unique in its view of citizenship. But it is less like Brazil or the United States today and more like, say, China, Qatar, Kuwait, Saudi Arabia, and Bhutan, all of which have strict immigration and naturalization policies designed to maintain a particular ethnic majority.

Back when a genuine two-state solution seemed like a possibility, I had always hoped that a Palestinian state, when or if it emerged alongside Israel, would be a state of all its citizens equally, and that it would welcome immigrants of all backgrounds. At that point, the failures to develop any kind of universalist vision of citizenship in Israel were far less import-ant to me than the idea that Israel could and should exist side-by-side with a genuine Palestinian state, one that made its own rules about rights and citizenship.

Now I believe that maybe all of us, globally, need to stop focusing on producing more and more nationalist states as the primary way of handling self-determination or the problem of oppressed minorities. The global community and its power bro-kers cannot continue to pull out "create a new state" as a go-to solution for ethnic or religious conflicts—as happened with the six new states born of former Yugoslavia in the early 1990s or when Eritrea was carved out of Ethiopia in 1993. The world's most recent state is South Sudan, which was founded in 2011 as a solution to a long-running civil war within Sudan. But it turned out there were major conflicts among the southern Sudanese themselves, and the young country soon descended itself into one of the world's most devasting civil wars. Is the solution ever smaller and more ethnically homogenous states?[196]

It is utopian, perhaps, to say we might be able to do better than the international state system that has ordered the world for the last two centuries, but I'm not alone in expressing it. The journalist Amjad Iraqi, for example, spoke recently on Klein's podcast about how important it is for us to begin to imagine a world beyond the nation-state as the container of our identities.[197] I am inspired by Malka Older's speculative near-future *Centenal Cycle* trilogy (2016–19), which tries to imagine global democracy without states.[198] Older pictures such a configuration as complex, problematic, and exciting. This kind of thinking is already happening in Israel and Palestine, too, where younger people are thinking critically about creative one-state or federated options for two peoples, neither of whom is going to leave the land.[199]

DECEMBER 22

The issue of sexual violence has been a weapon in the war of words for many weeks now. On the day of the Hamas attacks, according to Israeli accounts, a number of women and girls were raped and sexually assaulted. The physical evidence is limited, but there are some witness and also perpetrator accounts of sexual violence.[200] Israeli officials say that the lack of forensics is due to the fact that the emphasis of police and first responders was on collecting bodies for identification and quick burial, per Jewish custom. The pro-Palestinian side then raises doubts, points to inconsistencies in evidence or lack of women who have come forward. They underline the way that accusations of rape create a particular kind of rage, which is, unquestionably, being used to fuel support for the war.[201]

In general, the accusation of rape in war is not hard to believe. Rape has been used as a weapon of war in so many places: Bosnia, Congo, Nigeria, Iraq, Algeria, Rwanda... Men loosed on a battlefield, drunk with power and fear, commit rape because they can. Sometimes sexual violence is part of a war strategy, as it was when used against male prisoners during the civil war in El Salvador. But to prove that rape was a war crime by Hamas as an organization rather than something that individual fighters might have done, one has to prove it was ordered, planned, and systematic.

As Samah Salaime notes at +972, a magazine co-produced by Israelis and Palestinians, it will be a long time before we know exactly what happened on October 7. It often takes years for women to come forward. Salaime says she refuses to ignore the possibility that women were raped on October 7, either opportunistically or systematically, by Hamas or by hangers-on. Salaime is Palestinian citizen of Israel and she admits that "it would be much easier for me to immerse myself in videos of women being killed in Gaza, at least until the end of the war, to be a sharp Palestinian and a blurry feminist." But she will not, because turning away from what might have happened to some Israeli women and girls—to be a "blurry feminist"—would do a kind of violence to one of her deepest values.[202]

At the same time, we cannot ignore that the opposite also holds true. We have seen images of Palestinian men forced by Israeli soldiers to undress in the street—a sexualized form of ritual humiliation that Israelis say is designed to make sure no one has weapons.[203] There are other pictures of young male soldiers taking mocking selfies with Palestinian women's underwear. One would be naïve not to wonder what else might be happening to Palestinian females who are found alive and alone in Gaza.

DECEMBER 23

My favorite book by the brilliant novelist China Miéville is *The City & the City* (2009).[204] In this piece of speculative fiction, there is a murder that takes place in two fictional Eastern European cities at once: not on the border, exactly, because the two cities occupy the same space, the same streets. The citizens of the city-states of Besźel and Ul Qoma have somewhat different languages and very different religions, but they live side-by-side, sharing streets and parks. In order to live together but apart, they are trained not to see each other even when they are in the same space. "Unseeing" is a life-honed skill. They have to recognize the denizens that belong to the other city without actually *seeing* them.

The conceit could have been a simple allegory about race or religious difference, but what makes the novel work is its sustained and generous attention to what it takes to refuse to see that which is, literally, right beside you. The ideological work, the production of a certain self, and the lived reality of knowing what you cannot know: who is this person, right here on the same street, walking in a different city? Some of the buildings on the street are in your city, some are in theirs, you both know this and navigate it, perfectly. Sometimes a person makes a "breach" across the divide, intentional or not; the breachers disappear to unknown fates. The brilliance of the tale is that the distinctions don't feel ideological to the members of the two city states; they don't talk about the values of the other side, don't denigrate their fashion or their religion. The people are built, from birth onward, to perceive and live their bodies, their orientations, in a particular way—one that disallows seeing the other residents. That these two cities are the only place in the world like this—that this is, in fact, what makes the residents of these cities, together, like no one and nowhere else—is entirely lost on them.

Miéville imagines the hard work it takes to "unsee" the human reality that is right in front of us, the institutions and cultural work that reshape ordinary human connections into a distorted imaginary of separateness. He doesn't suggest that we can simply undo or deprogram these selves, but the novel does provide a sense that there is some basic connected truth about our lives amidst one another that we have to learn to "unsee." I'd like to think that this is more than sentimental humanism, but rather a form of asserting fundamental human living-in-relation. The plot pivots on a crime that has to be solved by police from each city; the story, though, is about ideology and what it might take to unlearn it.

Perhaps that unlearning is a matter of what Donna Haraway describes as "staying with the trouble"—that is, "learning to be truly present," not focusing our political narratives on fantasies of either "awful or edenic pasts" or "apocalyptic or salvific futures." These imagined havens or horrors make little room for the ordinary work of living in the mess of things. Instead, Haraway entreats us to concentrate on seeing ourselves "as mortal critters entwined in myriad unfinished configurations of places, times, matters, meanings."[205] That phrase "myriad unfinished configurations" gives me a kind of hope. Who knows where we are, along what timeline, in what unfinished process of historical unfolding?

DECEMBER 25

Bethlehem usually makes a big deal of Christmas. The place where tradition tells us that Jesus was born is also one of the few Christian holy places still under Palestinian control. Christmas is a high point, and the small city is decked out with a Christmas tree, extravagant decorations, and a large crèche in "Manger Square." There are multiple services and processions in order to accommodate the different sects: Catholic and Protestant services along with Greek Orthodox, Ethiopian, and Armenian. There are Santas and tourist shops with nativity scenes in olive wood.

The Palestinian Christian population is actually decreasing. In 1922, Christians were about 11% of the Arab population in the British mandate of Palestine. But the percentage of

Christians is less than 2% of the Palestinian population today, as Christians have emigrated at higher rates than Muslims.[206] In 2021, the Anglican Bishop in Jerusalem and the Archbishop of Canterbury penned an editorial decrying the increasing harassment of Christians and attacks on Christian sites by "radical elements" (settlers) who wanted to drive Christians out of Jerusalem.[207]

Bethlehem still enthusiastically makes itself into a pilgrimage site. Tourists from all over the world come to Israel and the West Bank. In 2019, before Covid, about 2.5 million Christians visited—more than half of total visitors.[208] Every tour group in Bethlehem has a Palestinian guide; the guides show them the Church of the Nativity, including the grotto in the basement where they believe the manger was. Often, guides try to weave into their narration a sense that Palestinians, no less than Israel, respect Christianity and its history.

This year, Christmas is different in Bethlehem. There is no tree-lighting ceremony. No decorations. The Evangelical Lutheran Church created a crèche but the baby Jesus is not lying in a makeshift cradle per the biblical story; instead the doll lies in a rubble of broken stones and tiles. "God is under the rubble in Gaza," the pastor says. "This is where we find God right now."[209]

DECEMBER 26

Despite my earlier doubts, I now think that it is reasonable to use the term "genocide," to describe what is happening in Gaza. Because making Gaza uninhabitable, killing whole families in targeted bombings, then using other bombs that can take out a city block—we have no better language for that than the term genocide. Israel is still making it almost impossible to get aid into Gaza: starvation is beginning to set in. The food is there, the medicine is there: sitting in trucks across the border in Egypt. Israel has developed an elaborate method for checking every truck, sending entire shipments back for no reason.

Two separate reports document the near-unprecedented level of damage done on Gaza. A major *Washington Post* investigation analyzes satellite imagery, airstrike data, and UN reports, alongside interviews with people on the ground and various experts. It concludes that "Israel has carried out its war in Gaza at a pace and a level of devastation that likely exceeds any recent conflict." In other words, Israel has destroyed more buildings and infrastructure than either the Syrian civil war from 2013 to 2016 or the US-led bombing campaign against the Islamic State in Syria and Iraq in 2017 (which killed 10,000 civilians). Another study by scholars at the City University of New York and Oregon State University came to similar conclusions, saying that Israel had likely destroyed two-thirds of the buildings in northern Gaza already.[210]

This is yet another record for this terrible war. The UN already announced last month that more of its humanitarian workers had been killed in Gaza than in any previous conflict.[211] This week, the US Committee to Protect Journalists has said that more journalists died in the first ten weeks of the Israel-Gaza war than in any single year of any conflict.[212]

I find it hard to even speculate on "the day after" because I wonder what "after" could possibly look like. Right now, 1% of the population of Gaza has been killed, but unevenly. Often entire families have died together. No part of the territory or the life there has been untouched. The concept of "rebuilding" an occupied and barricaded homeland seems obscene. Besides, Israel has already made clear that there will not be a "return" to the Gaza that was—a place already deeply overcrowded, under-resourced, and over-surveilled. Israel will never fully disappear Palestine, but Gaza will never be the same.

Gaza is slowly moving down the page of the *Washington Post* and the *New York Times*. Today there are two key stories, but they are located below musings about Trump and updates on the "challenge" China's national intelligence agency poses to the CIA. Gaza is now what we used to call "below the fold" back when people read newspapers in hard copy.

One story stands out: people inside Israel's establishment are growing more skeptical about Israel's ability to actually destroy Hamas. It is a mobile organization, large, able to replace one leader who is killed with another who is ready. And really, even if the thing called "Hamas" disappears, does anybody imagine that nothing else will rise to replace it? Will the eight-year-old boy who watches his grandmother die in a missile attack become an 18-year-old who is happy to accept Israel's control over his life? "Radicalizing a generation" seems to me the most obvious outcome of this war.

I have great admiration for the people in Palestine and Israel who fight hard to develop mutual recognition—not in the political sense, necessarily, but in the sense of actually being able to see each other's reality. There are a few of those folks. There are groups such the West-Eastern Divan Orchestra, composed of musicians from Israel, Palestine, and other Arab countries, founded by Edward Said and Daniel Barenboim; the Israeli group Standing Together, which includes Jewish Israelis and Palestinian citizens of Israel; the leftist cohort who run +972 magazine, which is named after the area code that both Israel and Palestine share.[213] Some people are determined to see each other as equals, to create partnerships, in a situation that mitigates against it at every turn. I once heard an Israeli colleague, Haggai Ram of Ben Gurion University of the Negev, comment that there were really only two places where Jews and Arabs interact together in relative equality. The first were gay bars. The second were gatherings where people smoked hashish or dope together.[214]

DECEMBER 29

At least 20,000 Gazans are dead, more than a quarter of them children, but the worst is yet to come. 85% of Gaza's population has been displaced. According to Devi Sridhar, the chair of global public health at the University of Edinburgh, Israel's talk of "safe zones" makes no sense unless those places are also made habitable. Right now, there is no clean water, no functional sanitation or toilets, not enough food, no access to adequate medical care. Children especially are at risk for diarrhea; the rates are already 100 times normal levels. Untreated, diarrhea can kill very quickly, especially in the young. There are serious worries about a cholera outbreak, given that sewage is untreated and floods risk putting that sewage into the small supplies of fresh water that exist.[215] Another physician says that approximately 40% of the children in Gaza are suffering from malnutrition.[216] It's often the case that the healthcare catastrophes downstream of conflict kill more people than bullets or bombs. Gaza is already under-resourced. With most of its infrastructure now destroyed, it could potentially lose 25% of its total population within the coming year.

DECEMBER 30

For the second time this month, the State Department bypasses Congress to approve emergency arms sales to Israel. This is different than the $18 billion aid package promised by the White House last month, which is for money to support the costs of the war, and it is in addition to the $106 million in arms sales that the State Department approved several weeks ago. Arms sales are not financial aid, but any arms sold by the US to another country are subject to review by Congress except in cases of emergency. The $147.5 million deal includes stuff—"fuses, chargers, and primers"—that will work with the rocket shells purchased earlier in the month. "Given the urgency of Israel's defensive needs," a State Department spokesperson said, "the secretary notified Congress that he [had determined] an emergency existed necessitating the immediate approval of the transfer."[217]

Josh Paul, a former State Department arms expert who resigned from his post in October to protest the US response to the war, told the *Washington Post* that the unguided weapons in these two packages allow Israel to continue with attacks that disproportionately kill civilians. He described the sales as "shameful."[218]

DECEMBER 31

It is so warm today in DC, again. The temperature is 50°F (10°C) outside. I find I cannot separate what is happening in Gaza from this reality of ongoing climate catastrophe. Partly that's because I'm reading about how Gazans are trying to deal with the winter, living outside, with little to protect them from the elements. Even in the Mediterranean, winter is harsh if you are homeless and hungry.

But there is another connection. It has something to do with timelines and what we have known and have chosen to ignore. Americans and Europeans, not just Israelis, have sat by for 70 years as things got worse and worse for Palestinians. We let it happen—because it was too hard, too complicated, because we had too much else to attend to. People could have known, the information was there in the refugee camps, in scholarly books, in the words of Palestinians themselves. Instead, people living in relative comfort saw terrorists or, at best, distant "refugees," while perhaps recalling the pretty pictures of Israel they saw at Sunday school or on a postcard.

During those same years, we knew about the destruction we have been leveling against the planet. The oil companies knew at least by the 1950s that what we were doing was unsustainable. The first Earth Day was in 1970; the Ozone crisis less than ten years later. Species extinction and pollution have been part of daily life for decades. Even now, as people in their twenties and younger are taking the fight to the streets, demanding immediate climate action, politicians and corporations come up with half-measures, 20-year plans. We are careening toward catastrophe—and in response, there are many seminars on the issue, even a new therapeutic specialization in climate despair.

If we manage to fight our way out of this and there are still historians around in a hundred years, perhaps they will use Miéville's novel to help them understand how we navigated the last several decades: by knowing, yet carefully refusing to see, the truth that has been all around us.

JANUARY 1, 2024

A US presidential election year. A year of environmental reckoning. A year of destruction in Gaza, as Netanyahu makes clear that the Israelis expect the war to continue for months.

Of course, I cannot know what 2024 will bring, in Palestine or the US or anywhere else. But a few things seem inevitable. There will be more floods and fires, more suffering. Millions of people across the world will die from preventable diseases, or hunger, or violence. There will also be friendship and laughter and new babies. There will be poetry.

Marcel Khalife and Mahmoud Darwish were both political artists, known for speaking "for" Palestine. Yet ultimately they both rebelled against the role, at least for a time. In the late 1990s, Khalife began making mostly instrumental music, beautiful symphonies that disengaged him from any overt pro-Palestinian content. It was only after the Arab spring in 2011 that he began to sing his pro-Palestine songs again, when a new future appeared, albeit briefly, on the horizon.

Darwish never lived to see that moment. He died of complications from heart surgery in 2008. But long before then he had begun to feel the burden of representation. Over time, his poetry has become self-consciously more difficult in its form, employing more complex language and rhythms and more abstract content, speaking more of myths and literature and less of politics and nation.[219] Still, he recognized and ultimately embraced that he would always be read as a political poet, as the voice of Palestine.

Every year there is a literary festival in Palestine, called PalFest, that brings artists from all over the world to Ramallah. In June 2008, the first year of the festival, Mahmoud Darwish wasn't able to attend because of heart problems. Instead, he sent a letter to the festival, which was read on opening night.

Part of it addressed the international participants in particular:

> Your courageous visit of solidarity is more than just a passing greeting to a people deprived of freedom and of a normal life; it is an expression of what Palestine has come to mean to the living human conscience that you represent. A literature born of a defined reality is able to create [...] an alternative, imagined reality. Not a search for a myth of happiness to flee from a brutal history, but an attempt [...] to transform us from victims of history, into partners in humanizing history.[220]

Less than three months later, Darwish died in Houston, Texas, from complications of heart surgery.

Darwish anticipated what we see happening in the pro-Palestinian movement today. One of the most striking things about the protests of fall 2023 is how much they seemed thick with history, with so many other political struggles just behind, still visible: Black Lives Matter; the demand for immigrant rights, for Queer and trans rights; the fight to save a deeply damaged if not doomed planet. In this moment, Palestine *has* come to represent and speak to the "living human conscience" that runs through it all, even as it is being battered from every corner.

If we follow Darwish's logic, Palestine matters because it is both specific and universal, both a land and a cause. It is a place as concrete as the flora and fauna that make that space between the river and the sea unique and as abstract as the basic humanity that links Palestinians to the larger world. Palestine was a home lost, very specifically, by people who still fight and suffer. But it is also a "cultural presence" that could help to "humanize history." Palestine stands today for itself, as a place of urgent political struggle, yet also resonates beyond itself: intertwined with—and a reminder of—every promise broken, every political injustice or erasure, every dream deferred.

On April 17, 2024, hundreds of students at Columbia University gathered with tents and posters to form an encampment in solidarity with Gaza on the campus. Their demands focused on getting the university to divest from corporations that "profit from Israeli apartheid, genocide, and occupation in Palestine." Following what would soon become a standard script, university president Minouche Shafik locked down the campus. Only Columbia ID holders could access the school. At 1 p.m. the next day, less than 36 hours after the protests began, Shafik asked the NYPD to arrest the protestors in order to secure "the safety of the community." [221] More than 100 people were arrested, their hands zip-tied as they were carried away in police buses. As the arrested students were removed from the lawn, several other people hopped the fence that had enclosed the demonstration area in order to repopulate the encampment. The message was clear: there are more of us than you can arrest.

Three days later, students began an encampment at the Massachusetts Institute of Technology in Cambridge, and protests then spread with stunning rapidity across the country: students were arrested at NYU and Yale on April 22, while protests and encampments were established at schools of every type, private and public, large and small, including Harvard, Northeastern, UCLA, Emory, Fordham, City College, and the University of Texas at Austin. By the middle of May, more than 60 colleges had student protest camps.

I was, by chance, in DC on Thursday, April 25. In the early morning hours, several dozen George Washington University students had gathered at University Lawn, setting up tents and beginning what would be a long encampment. I joined with other faculty from GW and other universities in DC to offer support for the students. As the day went on, more people came— soon there were several hundred, some in the encampment, some watching, some, like me, a little bit of both.

Throughout the day we were getting news of arrests around the country: students being led by the dozens or hundreds into police vans. An Emory college professor was thrown down on the ground by police. At the University of Texas, a professor who was supporting the students was handled brutally and ended up in the hospital with nine broken ribs.

GW's students were rowdy but joyous. There was a drummer standing just outside the campus boundary, accompanying the chants of "Free, Free Palestine" or "Divest! Divest! We will not stop, we will not rest." One student had put up a poster outside their tent listing all of the members of their family who had been killed by Israel—although the list of 161 people had become too long for the poster.

When I stopped by the encampment again on Sunday, it felt more like a folk festival than anything else. The students had been enclosed in their camp by the university: if they left, they could not return, and the GW administration "temporarily suspended" at least seven students, meaning they could not go to class, use the library, or get into their dorm rooms. But now many people from the community had come out and were sitting just next to the enclosures: right in the middle of H Street, a one-way road that ends about a block from the campus.

The street was filled with tents and tables laden with food and drinks. Families and young people congregated, greeting old friends and chatting. While I was there, the activity of the protest was focused on a do-it-yourself teach-in: at one end of the street, a young man in a keffiyeh was talking about a Palestinian novel that he found powerful. He was followed by an older Jewish man who talked about the history of the Israeli-Palestinian conflict. Later, when it became time for afternoon prayer for Muslims, the folks on the street made space and pulled out prayer mats. They asked those of us not praying to surround the prayer space—to provide protection, perhaps, but also to hide the prayers from prying eyes and media.

The night before, I had seen another set of prayers on Instagram. A GW student, a young Jewish man who had taken two of my classes, was talking to people at the GW protest about being Jewish, and the fact that he was proud, as a Jewish person, to be fighting for Palestine. He was even proud to be one of the students suspended in the service of a cause he believed in. He then turned to the person next to him, and they began to explain the seder service to the large group on H street. He described what the two candles stood for; other people began to hand out seder wine. The Jewish people in the crowd joined in the chanted prayer. There were many such chanters, because, as with so many times before, many Jewish people were at the front line of this movement.

You'd know that only if you looked for it: if you followed Jewish Voice for Peace on Instagram or watched the reporting from Al Jazeera. The majority of news and radio reports still posited this whole wave of protests as pitting Jewish students who felt unsafe on campus versus Palestinians or Arabs whose chanting was offensive or dangerous. TV and legacy media featured many interviews with Jewish students who said they felt afraid, that they were hearing antisemitism in the chants. I never heard antisemitism; although I did hear strong denouncements of Zionism, calls for revolution, demands for divestment from Israel, and prayers of many types.

Over the course of two weeks in April and May, more than 2,000 people were arrested in the United States in conjunction with the student protests. Very quickly, and in ways that few had anticipated, campuses had once again become a center of anti-war politics. It was clear that, for the first time in my lifetime, there were students and others—a large network of people from around the world—who were fully upholding Palestinian humanity. People who believed, unequivocally, that Palestinians have the right to complete equality: with Israelis, with everyone. "Free Palestine" was a commonplace slogan at sites from rallies to poetry readings, and that was something I had never expected to live to see.

Comparisons with Vietnam-era demonstrations were everywhere, but the anti-apartheid movement was a more direct parallel. Students and others in the 1980s had pioneered calls for divestment as a strategy, bringing their demands to the university: no financial gain from the suffering in South Africa. That activism had set the tone of this generation's occupation of space and their calls for divestment from companies that benefited from Israel's destruction of Palestinian life.

Palestinians on the ground responded with generosity and gratitude to the remarkable wave of student commitment. A teacher in Gaza posted images of their students holding up placards with the names of US universities where there were protests. The Palestinian journalist Hind Khoudary included a tribute on her Instagram page.

For every student protesting in the USA:
I see you. I hear you.
I am more than proud of every one of you.
Thanks for speaking and protesting for Palestine.
Thanks for proving to the world that our generation is going
to bring change to the world.

On May 14, Harvard's encampment peacefully ended after students negotiated with the Harvard administration a "discussion" about both the possibility of divestment and about the ways Palestinian issues were taught on campus. At UC Riverside, there was a much more robust agreement to pursue divestment.

At GW, the administration sent in police to clear the encampment in the middle of the night, and several students were arrested. Two days later, students regathered in front of the university president's home, singing and dancing until the police were called. This time, they dispersed, but made clear they would gather again and again, as needed. Two days later, they were invited to a meeting with GW's administration.

Clearly, this movement of students is indicative of a crucial generational change in views toward Palestine and the willingness of people to be critical of Israel. It is also connected to the multiple crises of the last five years: the isolation and economic costs of Covid, the killing of Black people by police that led to Black Lives Matter, the children separated from their parents at the Mexican border, the rise of a populist and overtly racist right wing under the banner of Trumpism, and perhaps, the deepening awareness of our already-underway climate disaster. (Compared to the billions of dollars the Biden administration has given to weapons for Israel, our climate response looks anemic—the $16 billion aid package that Biden promised Israel is equal to almost the entire federal budget for renewable energy support in fiscal year 2022.[222]) It is no wonder that, watching

Israel's bombing of Gaza, and the determined way in which it has destroyed people, hospitals, schools, and animals, young people simply refuse to accept yet another attack on the basics of human dignity and global survival.

The students are not alone. The movement for Palestine includes many millions of people of diverse backgrounds and different generations. It is happening not just in the US or Europe, but around the world.

And yet: in Gaza, people were still being bombed as Israel invaded the southern town of Rafah. In the north, Gaza was stricken by full-blown famine, with people eating leaves and scraps as much aid remained trapped at the Israeli border.[223] By early April, the number of children that had been killed by Israel in the Gaza war was greater than the total number of children killed in all conflicts globally from 2019 to 2022.[224]

Journalism has remained under threat at every level. By May 1, more journalists had been killed in the Gaza war than any conflict since the Committee to Protect Journalists began gathering data in 1992. More than 75% of all journalists killed anywhere in 2023 were killed in Gaza.[225] On May 5, Israel shut down Al Jazeera's Israel office, withdrew its crew accreditations, and banned media services from transmitting its broadcasts.

There is danger at every turn: the destruction of Gaza's infrastructure is all but complete, yet most of the people remain, steadfast, in their territory. I greatly fear that the most likely outcome of this war is stalemate. Israel will eventually declare victory and leave the field, pulling back most of its troops but leaving a strong military and policing presence in Gaza. (Or perhaps it will be able to outsource that job to Egypt.) There will be no attempts to restore Palestinian self-governance in the Strip. Gazans will bury their dead, try to rebuild their homes, try to find a way. And anyone who can get out will do so, leaving fewer Palestinians for Israel to rule. Humanitarian organizations will be allowed to try to regroup, offer some forms of development, which over time *might* bring Gaza back to the level of impoverishment in which it existed before October 2023.

I hope I'm wrong. I hope the global protests will continue to demand justice, and manage to actually achieve it, even once the violence becomes less visible—slow rather than fast, routine rather than spectacular. Our track record is not good on this score. But the time for a planetary consciousness is now, and we have an example of what such consciousness looks like. I hope we can find a way to make something hopeful in the wake of all this death—not just a story, but a story of transformation.

FOOTNOTES

1   As of May 1, 2024, 35,000 people had been killed and over 70,000 injured according to Gaza's Health Ministry and the United Nations.

2   John Berger, *Ways of Seeing: Based on the BBC Television Series* (London: Penguin Books, 1990).

3   *Marcel Khalifé "Voyageur,"* 2004, www.youtube.com/watch?v=ksIVefQjiCA

4   Throughout the book, I use the term "Middle East" or sometimes "the Middle East and North Africa" (MENA) when I want to refer broadly to events or issues that cover several countries in the region. Today many scholars prefer SWANA (South West Asia and North Africa) over MENA, since the "Middle East" is a term coined by looking from Europe. No matter which term one chooses, the exact definition varies. The US-based Middle East Studies Association has an expansive view: the organization "is primarily concerned with the area encompassing Iran, Turkey, Afghanistan, Pakistan, and the countries of the Arab World (and their diasporas)." This definition includes North Africa, but most scholars now use MENA to make the definition more explicit. I use both, or name specific countries when that is most appropriate.

5   Lucy Kurtzer-Ellenbogen et al., "Is a Saudi-Israel Normalization Agreement on the Horizon?" (Washington, DC: United States Institute of Peace, September 28, 2023), www.usip.org/publications/2023/09/saudi-israel-normalization-agreement-horizon

6   1,189 people were killed, including 796 Israeli civilians (including 71 foreigners) and 379 Israeli security forces. This count from May 2024 includes 37 hostages whose deaths have since been confirmed. AFP-Agence France Presse, "New Tally Puts Oct 7 Attack Death Toll In Israel At 1,189," *Barron's*, May 24, 2024, www.barrons.com/news/new-tally-puts-oct-7-attack-death-toll-in-israel-at-1-189-3e038de6

7   Alan Pino, "What Was Hamas Thinking? And What Is It Thinking Now?," *Atlantic Council* (blog), October 16, 2023, www.atlanticcouncil.org/blogs/new-atlanticist/what-was-hamas-thinking-and-what-is-it-thinking-now/; Adam Rasgon and David D. Kirkpatrick, "What Was Hamas Thinking?," *The New Yorker*, October 13, 2023, www.newyorker.com/news/news-desk/what-was-hamas-thinking; Azzam Shaath and Reham Owda, "Hamas' October Attacks and the Israeli War on Gaza: Reflections from Palestinians," Carnegie Endowment for International Peace, October 24, 2023, www.carnegieendowment.org/sada/90836

8   Associated Press, "U.N.: Over 200 Palestinians and Nearly 30 Israelis Killed in 2023," *Spectrum News*, August 21, 2023, www.ny1.com/nyc/all-boroughs/international/2023/08/21/this-year-over-200-palestinians-and-nearly-30-israelis-have-been-killed--highest-since-2005--un-says

9   Amira Hass, "Israel Holds Up Vital Spare Parts for Gaza's Water and Sewage Systems," *Ha'aretz*, January 9, 2022, www.haaretz.com/israel-news/2022-01-09/ty-article/.premium/israel-holds-up-vital-spare-parts-for-gazas-water-and-sewagesystems/0000017f-e7eb-d97e-a37f-f7efd5c50000

10   Sara Roy, *Unsilencing Gaza: Reflections on Resistance* (London: Pluto Press, 2021).

11   Noura Erakat, "The Violence of Demanding Perfect Victims," *Jadaliyya*, October 10, 2023, www.jadaliyya.com/Details/45383/The-violence-of-demanding-perfect-victims

12   Palestine Campaign for Human Rights and B'Tselem, "Unwilling and Unable: Israel's Whitewashed Investigations of the Great March of Return Protests" (Jerusalem, December 2021), www.btselem.org/publications/202112_unwilling_and_unable; Tareq Hajjaj, "Five Years on, Gaza's Great March of Return Changed People's Lives," *Mondoweiss*, March 30, 2023, mondoweiss.net/2023/03/five-years-on-gazas-great-march-of-return-changed-peoples-lives/; MSF, "Shattered Limbs, Shattered Lives: Great March of Return," Médecins Sans Frontières (MSF) International, www.msf.org/great-march-return-depth

13   Langston Hughes, "Harlem," in Langston Hughes, *The Collected Poems of Langston Hughes*, ed. Arnold Rampersad, annotated edition (New York: Vintage, 1995).

14   The White House, "Remarks by President Biden on the Terrorist Attacks in Israel," The White House, October 10, 2023, www.whitehouse.gov/briefing-room/speeches-remarks/2023/10/10/remarks-by-president-biden-on-the-terrorist-attacks-in-israel-2/

15   Belkis Wille and Birgit Schwartz, "Interview: Building the Evidence for Crimes Committed in Israel on October 7" (New York: Human Rights Watch, January 31, 2024), www.hrw.org/news/2024/01/31/interview-building-evidence-crimes-committed-israel-october-7

16   Aaron Boxerman, "What We Know About the Death Toll in Israel From the Hamas-Led Attacks," *The New York Times*, November 12, 2023, www.nytimes.com/2023/11/12/world/middleeast/israel-death-toll-hamas-attack.html; Linda Dayan and Maya Lecker, "How Haaretz Is Counting Israel's Dead from the October 7 Hamas Attack," *Haaretz*, November 23, 2023, www.haaretz.com/haaretz-explains/2023-11-23/ty-article-magazine/.premium/how-haaretz-is-counting-israels-dead-from-the-october-7-hamas-attack/0000018b-d42c-d423-affb-f7afe1a70000

17   Later investigations revealed no evidence of beheaded children, although babies were definitely among those killed. Maureen Tkacik, "What Really Happened on October 7?," *The American Prospect*, March 20, 2024, www.prospect.org/api/content/604afa20-e6fe-11ee-90f2-12163087a831/

18   Boxerman, "What We Know About the Death Toll in Israel From the Hamas-Led Attacks," *The New York Times*, November 12, 2023, www.nytimes.com/2023/11/12/world/middleeast/israel-death-toll-hamas-attack.html

19   "Damning Evidence of War Crimes as Israeli Attacks Wipe out Entire Families in Gaza," Amnesty International, October 20, 2023, www.amnesty.org/en/latest/news/2023/10/damning-evidence-of-war-crimes-as-israeli-attacks-wipe-out-entire-families-in-gaza/

20   Mahmoud Darwish, *'Aṣāfīr Bi-Lā Ajniḥa (Wingless Birds)* (Beirut: Dār al-'Awda, 1960); Mahmoud Darwish, *Awraq Al-Zaytun (Olive Leaves)* (Haifa: Maṭba'at al-Ittiḥād al-Ta'āwunīyah, 1964). The poem "Identity Card" has appeared in a number of English collections of Darwish's poetry, including Mahmoud Darwish, *The Music of Human Flesh*, Arab Authors 7 (London: Washington, D.C.: Heinemann: Three Continents Press, 1980).

21   Shira Robinson, *Citizen Strangers: Palestinians and the Birth of Israel's Liberal Settler State* (Stanford: Stanford University Press, 2013).

22   Khaled Mattawa, *Mahmoud Darwish: The Poet's Art and His Nation* (Syracuse: Syracuse University Press, 2014), 7–9. There are many translations of the poem, but I prefer Mattawa's elegant rendition.

23   Mattawa, *Mahmoud Darwish*, 14–29.

24   Emma Bowman and Laura Wamsley, "Tens of Thousands Gather for Pro-Palestinian March in D.C. to Demand Gaza Cease-Fire," *NPR*, Washington, DC, November 4, 2023, www.npr.org/2023/11/04/1210669096/palestine-march-washington-dc-cease-fire-israel-protest-gaza

25   Jessica Winegar, "Egypt: A Multigenerational Revolt," *Jadaliyya*, February 21, 2011, www.jadaliyya.com/Details/23721/Egypt-A-Multi-Generational-Revolt

26   Ari Daniel, "Doctors in Gaza Describe the War's Devastating Impact on Health Care — and Civilians," *NPR*, October 13, 2023, www.npr.org/sections/goatsandsoda/2023/10/13/1203503616/doctors-in-gaza-describe-the-wars-devastating-impact-on-hospitals-and-health-car

27   Arwa Ibrahim, Edna Mohamed, and Joseph Stepansky, "Israel-Hamas Updates: 45 Killed in Israel Strike on Gaza Apartment Block," *Al Jazeera*, October 11, 2023, www.aljazeera.com/news/liveblog/2023/10/11/israel-hamas-war-live-gaza-faces-growing-humanitarian-catastrophe

28   See for example Joan Peters, *From Time Immemorial: The Origins of the Arab-Jewish Conflict over Palestine* (Chicago: JKAP Publications, 2001).

29   "Situation Report #6 on the Gaza Strip & the West Bank," UNRWA, October 16, 2023, www.unrwa.org/resources/reports/situation-report-6-gaza-strip-west-bank

30   See my discussion of these events in Melani McAlister, *Epic Encounters: Culture, Media, and U.S. Interests in the Middle East Since 1945*, 2nd ed. (Berkeley: University of California Press, 2005).

31   Paul Chamberlin, *The Global Offensive: The United States, the Palestine Liberation Organization, and the Making of the Post-Cold War Order* (Oxford: Oxford University Press, 2012); Avraham Sela, "The PLO at Fifty: A Historical Perspective," *Contemporary Review of the Middle East* (Online) 1, no. 3 (2014): 269–333.

32   A. J. McDougall, "'Doxxing Truck' Circles Harvard After Students Sign Pro-Palestine Letter," *The Daily Beast*, October 12, 2023, www.thedailybeast.com/doxxing-truck-circles-harvard-after-students-sign-letter-blaming-israel-for-hamas-attacks

33   Eren Orbey, "The Anguished Fallout from a Pro-Palestinian Letter at Harvard," *The New Yorker*, October 20, 2023, www.newyorker.com/news/dispatch/the-anguished-fallout-from-a-pro-palestinian-letter-at-harvard

34   For a complex conversation and a fascinating, evolving take on this argument, see Judith Butler, "The Compass of Mourning," *London Review of Books*, October 19, 2023, www.lrb.co.uk/the-paper/v45/n20/judith-butler/the-compass-of-mourning; also Naomi Klein, "In Gaza and Israel, Side with the Child over the Gun," *The Guardian*, October 11, 2023, www.theguardian.com/commentisfree/2023/oct/11/why-are-some-of-the-left-celebrating-the-killings-of-israeli-jews

35   Dread Scott, "Shall I Condemn Myself a Little for You?," *Hyperallergic*, October 20, 2023, www.hyperallergic.com/851975/shall-i-condemn-myself-a-little-for-you/

36   However, several important commentaries have used international
      law to make crucial arguments. For a pro-Palestinian perspective see
      Deborah Chasman and Noura Erakat, "The Crimes Are Plenty," *Boston
      Review*, October 13, 2023, www.bostonreview.net/articles/the-crimes-
      are-plenty/; Noura Erakat, *Justice for Some: Law and the Question of
      Palestine* (Stanford: Stanford University Press, 2019). For a perspective
      supporting Israel, see David J. Scheffer, "What International Law Has
      to Say About the Israel-Hamas War," Council on Foreign Relations,
      October 19, 2023, www.cfr.org/article/what-international-law-has-say-
      about-israel-hamas-war

37   L. Ali Khan, "Academic Freedom Under Attack: The Chilling Effect
      of Surveillance Sites on US Professors Who Criticize Israel," *JURIST:
      Legal News*, November 20, 2023, www.jurist.org/commentary/2023/11/
      academic-freedom-under-attack-the-chilling-effect-of-anonymous-
      surveillance-sites-on-us-professors/

38   Brian Bushard, "Billionaire Ackman, Others Pledge They Won't
      Hire Harvard Students Who Signed Letter Blaming Israel For
      Hamas Attack," *Forbes*, October 11, 2023, www.forbes.com/sites/
      brianbushard/2023/10/10/billionaire-ackman-others-pledge-they-
      wont-hire-harvard-students-who-signed-letter-criticizing-israel/; Pierre
      Paulden, "Billionaire Bill Ackman Argues His Antisemitism Crusade
      against Harvard Is Totally Unrelated to His 'Unfortunate Experience as
      a Donor,'" *Fortune*, December 13, 2023, www.fortune.com/2023/12/13/
      bill-ackman-harvard-donation-coupang-antisemitism-president/; Peter
      Rudegeair, "Bill Ackman's Clash With Harvard Over Stock Gift Reveals
      the Messy World of Big Donations," *The Wall Street Journal*, December
      13, 2023, www.wsj.com/us-news/education/bill-ackmans-clash-with-
      harvard-over-stock-gift-reveals-the-messy-world-of-big-donations-
      2d12dc4b

39   Middle East Studies Association's Committee on Academic Freedom,
      "Letter to Troy McKenzie, Dean of NYU Law School," October
      17, 2023, www.mesana.org/advocacy/committee-on-academic-
      freedom/2023/10/17/letter-protesting-threats-to-ryna-workmans-
      academic-freedom

40   "Israel-Hamas War: Piers Morgan vs Bassem Youssef On Palestine's
      Treatment," *Piers Morgan Uncensored* (Fox Nation, October 17, 2023),
      www.youtube.com/watch?v=4idQbwsvtUo

41   Jaclyn Diaz and Alana Wise, "From Amman to D.C., Protests Erupt for
      Palestinians Following the Gaza Hospital Blast," *NPR*, October 18, 2023,
      www.npr.org/2023/10/18/1206893627/from-amman-to-d-c-protests-
      erupt-for-palestinians-following-the-gaza-hospital-bl; "Biden Lands
      in Israel, Hugs Netanyahu and Herzog on Tarmac," *Reuters*, October
      18, 2023, www.reuters.com/world/biden-lands-israel-consult-gaza-
      war-2023-10-18/

42   Mahmoud Darwish, *The End of the Night - Akheer Al Leel* (Beirut, 1967).

43   Marcel Khalife, *Promises of the Storm*, Paredon Records, 1983.

44   Jean Said Makdisi, *Beirut Fragments: A War Memoir* (New York: Persea Books, 1990).

45   Rashid Khalidi, *The Hundred Years' War on Palestine: A History of Settler Colonialism and Resistance, 1917–2017*, Illustrated edition (New York: Metropolitan Books, 2020), 142. The quote is from former Israeli Chief of Staff Mordechi Gur, speaking to a secret session of the Knesset Defense and Foreign Affairs committee in 1982.

46   Sarah E. Parkinson, "The Ghosts of Lebanon," *Foreign Affairs*, November 14, 2023, www.foreignaffairs.com/israel/ghosts-lebanon; Khalidi, *The Hundred Years' War on Palestine*.

47   Robin Wright, "Another Siege: Israel's War on the P.L.O.," *The New Yorker*, August 2, 2014, www.newyorker.com/news/news-desk/another-summer-another-siege-israels-war-p-l-o

48   Amy Kaplan, *Our American Israel: The Story of an Entangled Alliance* (Cambridge, MA: Harvard University Press, 2018), 136–45.

49   The exact death toll is still not known. The IDF figure is 700. Lebanese historian Bayan Nuwayhed al-Hout used ethnographic methods to estimate approximately 1,400 dead or missing in *Sabra and Shatila: September 1982* (London: Pluto Press, 2004). Lebanese authorities published a figure of 2,000 shortly after the war. The journalist Amnon Kapeliouk estimated 3,000–3,500 in *Sabra and Shatila: Inquiry into a Massacre* (AAUG Press, 1984).

50   Kaplan, *Our American Israel*, 136.

51   Ilana Feldman, *Life Lived in Relief: Humanitarian Predicaments and Palestinian Refugee Politics* (Oakland: University of California Press, 2018).

52   Kaplan, *Our American Israel*, 3ff.

53   Lisa Lowe, *The Intimacies of Four Continents* (Durham: Duke University Press Books, 2015); Saidiya Hartman, *Lose Your Mother: A Journey Along the Atlantic Slave Route*, (New York: Farrar, Straus and Giroux, 2008).

54   Chimamanda Ngozi Adichie, *Half of a Yellow Sun* (New York: Anchor, 2007).

55   Aimee Dawson, "Tate's Huge 'Guernica of the Arab World' is Recreated in Tapestry So it Can Travel the World," *The Art Newspaper*, September 19, 2019, www.theartnewspaper.com/2019/09/19/tates-huge-guernica-of-the-arab-world-is-recreated-in-tapestry-so-it-can-travel-the-world

56   David Scott, *Conscripts of Modernity: The Tragedy of Colonial Enlightenment*, (Durham: Duke University Press Books, 2004).

57   Scott, *Conscripts of Modernity*, 29–31.

58   Marc Matera, *Black London: The Imperial Metropolis and Decolonization in the Twentieth Century* (Berkeley: University of California Press, 2015); Kennetta Hammond Perry, *London is the Place for Me: Black Britons, Citizenship and the Politics of Race* (New York: Oxford University Press, 2016); Gary Wilder, *The French Imperial Nation-State: Negritude and Colonial Humanism between the Two World Wars* (Chicago: University of Chicago Press, 2005).

59   Scott, *Conscripts of Modernity*, 29.

60   Karl Marx and Friedrich Engels, "The Eighteenth Brumaire of Louis Bonaparte," in *The Communist Manifesto and Other Writings*, trans. Martin Puchner (New York: Barnes & Noble Classics, 2009).

61   "Israel-Hamas War: List of Key Events, Day 18," *Al Jazeera*, www.aljazeera.com/news/2023/10/24/israel-hamas-war-list-of-key-events-day-18

62   *Surgery Without Supplies in Gaza: "You Cannot Imagine,"* 2023, www.youtube.com/watch?v=HwZ0l2lzjJg

63   Zachary Lockman, *Comrades and Enemies: Arab and Jewish Workers in Palestine, 1906–1948* (Berkeley: University of California Press, 1996).

64   Noura Erakat, *Justice for Some: Law and the Question of Palestine* (Stanford: Stanford University Press, 2019), 22–60.

65   Eugene L. Rogan and Avi Shlaim (eds.), *The War for Palestine: Rewriting the History of 1948*, 2nd edition (New York: Cambridge University Press, 2007).

66   Adam Hanieh, "The Internationalisation of Gulf Capital and Palestinian Class Formation," *Capital & Class* 35, no. 1 (February 2011): 81–106.

67   "Demographics," Arab American Institute, May 2024, www.aaiusa.org/demographics

68   Eventually, in 2005, the Jewish settlements in Gaza were dismantled and the army were evacuated.

69   Government of Israel and Palestinian Delegation, "UN Document Security Council Document S/26560: Declaration of Principles on Interim Self-Government Arrangements" (United Nations, October 11, 1993).

70   Wendy Orange, *Coming Home To Jerusalem: A Personal Journey* (New York: Simon & Schuster, 2001), 114–16.

71   Graham Usher, "Why Gaza Says Yes, Mostly," in *Dispatches from Palestine: The Rise and Fall of the Oslo Peace Process* (London: Pluto Press, 1999), 12–17, www.jstor.org/stable/j.ctt18fsbd1.6; Farah Najjar, "'Olive Branches, Victory Signs': How the Oslo Accords Failed the Palestinians," *The Washington Report on Middle East Affairs* 42, no. 7 (2023): 41–43.

72   Khalidi, *The Hundred Years' War on Palestine*, 199.

73   Khalidi, *The Hundred Years' War on Palestine*, 193.

74   Edward Said, "The Morning After," *London Review of Books*, October 21, 1993, www.lrb.co.uk/the-paper/v15/n20/edward-said/the-morning-after

75   Tamer Qarmout and Daniel Béland, "The Politics of International Aid to the Gaza Strip," *Journal of Palestine Studies* 41, no. 4 (2012): 32–47; UNRWA, "Gaza_15 Years of Blockade" (UNRWA, 2022), www.unrwa. org/gaza15-years-blockade

76   Mairav Zonszein, "Israel Killed More Palestinians in 2014 than in Any Other Year since 1967," *The Guardian*, March 27, 2015, www.theguardian.com/world/2015/mar/27/israel-kills-more-palestinians-2014-than-any-other-year-since-1967; Ido Zelkovitz, "A Paradise Lost? The Rise and Fall of the Palestinian Community in Kuwait," *Middle Eastern Studies* 50, no. 1 (2014): 86–99.

77   Roy, *Unsilencing Gaza*, 111.

78   As of February 1, 2024, the official Israeli figures of those killed by Hamas were 767 civilians, 20 hostages, and 376 members of the security forces, giving a total of 1,163. Agence France Presse, "New Tally Puts October 7 Attack Dead In Israel At 1,163," *Barron's*, February 1, 2024, www.barrons.com/news/new-tally-puts-october-7-attack-dead-in-israel-at-1-163-78182279

79   Hammad is the author of several volumes of poetry, including Suheir Hammad, *Born Palestinian, Born Black* (New York: Writers & Readers, 1996).

80   Suheir Hammad, "First Writing Since," *Middle East Report*, no. 221 (2001): 2–3.

81   Hannah Hartig and Carroll Doherty, "Two Decades Later, the Enduring Legacy of 9/11" (Washington, DC: Pew Research Center) September 2, 2021, www.pewresearch.org/politics/2021/09/02/two-decades-later-the-enduring-legacy-of-9-11/

82   Stephanie Savell, "How Death Outlives War: The Reverberating Impact of the Post-9/11 Wars on Human Health" (Brown University: Costs of War Project, May 15, 2023), watson.brown.edu/costsofwar/papers/2023/IndirectDeaths

83   Matt Horton, "Poets Suheir Hammad and Nathalie Handal, Musician Marcel Khalifé Light Up the Kennedy Center," *Washington Report on Middle East Affairs* 28, no. 4 (June 5, 2009): 61–62.

84   Shira Rubin and William Booth, "Early Stages of Israeli Ground Assault in Gaza Shrouded in Secrecy," *The Washington Post*, October 30, 2023, www.washingtonpost.com/world/2023/10/29/israel-ground-war-gaza/; Wafaa Shurafa, Bassem Mroue, and Josef Federman, "Israel Steps up Air and Ground Attacks in Gaza and Cuts off the Territory's Communications," *AP News*, October 28, 2023, www.apnews.com/article/israel-palestinians-gaza-airstrikes-region-e41b5b12e8cdf9db62395314d9a782b6

85   Pamela E. Pennock, *The Rise of the Arab American Left: Activists, Allies, and Their Fight against Imperialism and Racism, 1960s–1980s* (Chapel Hill: The University of North Carolina Press, 2017); Salim Yaqub, *Imperfect Strangers: Americans, Arabs, and U.S.-Middle East Relations in the 1970s* (Ithaca: Cornell University Press, 2016). On the developing cultural awareness among Arab Americans, see Sarah M. A. Gualtieri, *Arab Routes: Pathways to Syrian California* (Stanford: Stanford University Press, 2019).

86   Letter to the Editor, *Sojourner* magazine, March 1982, 2.

87   Sam Roberts, "Meron Benvenisti Dies at 86; Urged One State for Jews and Palestinians," *The New York Times*, September 29, 2020, www.nytimes.com/2020/09/29/world/meron-benvenisti-dead.html; Meron Benvenisti, "The Turning Point in Israel," *The New York Review of Books*, October 13, 1983, www.nybooks.com/articles/1983/10/13/the-turning-point-in-israel/

88   The census rules remain the same, but the sentiment of MENA populations is changing. See Karen Zraick et al., "No Box to Check: When the Census Doesn't Reflect You," *The New York Times*, February 25, 2024, www.nytimes.com/interactive/2024/02/25/us/census-race-ethnicity-middle-east-north-africa.html

89   McAlister, *Epic Encounters*.

90   Saree Makdisi, *Tolerance Is a Wasteland: Palestine and the Culture of Denial* (Oakland: University of California Press, 2022); Kaplan, *Our American Israel*; Shaul Mitelpunkt, *Israel in the American Mind: The Cultural Politics of US-Israeli Relations, 1958–1988* (Cambridge: Cambridge University Press, 2018); Michelle Mart, *Eye on Israel: How America Came to View Israel As an Ally* (Albany: State University of New York Press, 2007).

91   Jonathan Masters and Will Merrow, "U.S. Aid to Israel in Four Charts," Council on Foreign Relations, May 31, 2024, www.cfr.org/article/us-aid-israel-four-charts

92   Stephen Zunes, "How US Policy Has Empowered Hamas," *Common Dreams*, November 1, 2023, www.commondreams.org/opinion/us-policy-empowered-hamas

93   "Hostilities in the Gaza Strip and Israel - Reported Impact | Day 29," United Nations Office for the Coordination of Humanitarian Affairs - occupied Palestinian territory, November 4, 2023, www.ochaopt.org/content/hostilities-gaza-strip-and-israel-reported-impact-day-29

94   Roxana Saberi, "Israel Releases Graphic Video of Hamas Terror Attacks as Part of 'Narrative Battle' over War in Gaza," *CBS News*, October 26, 2023, www.cbsnews.com/news/israel-video-of-hamas-terror-attacks-war-in-gaza/

95   Barbara Schabowska and Monika Gabriela Bartoszewicz, "Edward W. Said: Not so Lost Reflections *On Lost Causes* Such as the One-State Solution," *Global Change, Peace & Security*, July 24, 2024, 1–17.

96   Bowman and Wamsley, "Tens of Thousands Gather for Pro-Palestinian
      March in D.C. to Demand Gaza Cease-Fire," *NPR*, November 4, 2023,
      www.npr.org/2023/11/04/1210669096/palestine-march-washington-dc-
      cease-fire-israel-protest-gaza

97   Mairav Zonszein, "Settler Violence Rises in the West Bank during
      the Gaza War," International Crisis Group, November 6, 2023, www.
      crisisgroup.org/middle-east-north-africa/east-mediterranean-mena/
      israelpalestine/settler-violence-rises-west-bank-gaza-war; Shane Bauer,
      "The Israeli Settlers Attacking Their Palestinian Neighbors," *The New
      Yorker*, February 26, 2024, www.newyorker.com/magazine/2024/03/04/
      israel-west-bank-settlers-attacks-palestinians

98   Isabel DeBre, "2 Palestinian Gunmen Kill at Least 4 at a Gas Station
      near Israeli West Bank Settlement," *PBS NewsHour*, June 20, 2023,
      www.pbs.org/newshour/world/palestinian-gunman-kills-at-least-4-at-
      a-gas-station-near-israeli-west-bank-settlement

99   Omar Baddar, "Israel Is Committing War Crimes in Gaza—and the U.S.
      Is Supporting It," *Newsweek*, October 25, 2023, www.newsweek.com/
      israel-committing-war-crimes-gaza-us-supporting-it-opinion-1837908

100   Krystal Kyle, "Episode 148: Omar Baddar," *Krystal Kyle and Friends*,
      November 4, 2023, krystalkyleandfriends.substack.com/p/episode-148-
      audio-omar-baddar

101   Jon B. Alterman, "Israel Could Lose," *Center for Strategic and
      International Studies* (blog), November 7, 2023, www.csis.org/analysis/
      israel-could-lose

102   Amaney A. Jamal and Michael Robbins, "What Palestinians
      Really Think of Hamas," *Foreign Affairs*, October 25, 2023,
      www.foreignaffairs.com/israel/what-palestinians-really-think-hamas

103   Arab World for Research and Development, "Public Opinion Polls:
      Gaza Survey 7th October" (Ramallah, Palestine, November 14, 2023),
      www.awrad.org/files/server/polls/polls2023/Public%20Opinion%20
      Poll%20-%20Gaza%20War%202023%20-%20Tables%20of%20
      Results.pdf

104   "A Statement by Journalists," Protect Journalists, November 9, 2023,
      www.protect-journalists.com; Laura Wagner and Will Sommer,
      "Hundreds of Journalists Sign Letter Protesting Coverage of Israel," *The
      Washington Post*, November 13, 2023, www.washingtonpost.com/style/
      media/2023/11/09/open-letter-journalists-israel-gaza/

105   Maya Yang, "Islamophobia and Antisemitism on Rise in US amid
      Israel-Hamas War," *The Guardian*, November 10, 2023, www.
      theguardian.com/us-news/2023/nov/10/us-islamophobia-antisemitism-
      hate-speech-israel-hamas-war-gaza; Ismail Allison, "CAIR Received
      1,283 Complaints Over Past Month, an 'Unprecedented' Increase in
      Complaints of Islamophobia, Anti-Arab Bias," November 9, 2023,
      www.cair.com/press_releases/cair-received-1283-complaints-over-past-

month-an-unprecedented-increase-in-complaints-of-islamophobia-anti-arab-bias/

106   George Hawley, *Making Sense of the Alt-Right* (New York: Columbia
       University Press, 2017); Tamir Bar-On, "The Alt-Right's Continuation of
       the 'Cultural War' in Euro-American Societies," *Thesis Eleven* 163, no.
       1 (2021): 43–70; Cynthia Miller-Idriss, *Hate in the Homeland: The New
       Global Far Right* (Princeton: Princeton University Press, 2022).

107   Jeff Diamant, "Anti-Jewish Harassment Occurred in 94 Countries in
       2020, up from Earlier Years," *Pew Research Center* (blog), March 17, 2023,
       www.pewresearch.org/short-reads/2023/03/17/anti-jewish-harassment-
       occurred-in-94-countries-in-2020-up-from-earlier-years/; "EXCLUSIVE:
       CNN Poll Reveals Depth of Anti-Semitism in Europe," November 2018,
       www.cnn.com/interactive/2018/11/europe/antisemitism-poll-2018-intl

108   "ADL Records Dramatic Increase in U.S. Antisemitic Incidents
       Following Oct. 7 Hamas Massacre," Anti-Defamation League, October
       24, 2023, www.adl.org/resources/press-release/adl-records-dramatic-
       increase-us-antisemitic-incidents-following-oct-7

109   Judith Butler, "On Antisemitism," in *A Field Guide to White Supremacy*
       (Berkeley: University of California Press, 2021), 160–68.

110   The International Holocaust Remembrance Alliance developed a brief
       working definition of antisemitism in 2016, but its webpage circulates
       the definition with a list of eleven "examples" that are much more
       far-ranging than the definition itself. www.holocaustremembrance.com/
       resources/working-definition-antisemitism

111   See, for example, "Statement from Concerned Jewish Faculty
       Against Antisemitism," signed by more than 1300 scholars as of
       May 25, 2024, at www.concernedjewishfaculty.org/about/. The
       Middle East Studies Association has also strongly criticized this
       definition. "What is Antisemitism?," *IHRA* (blog), May 26, 2016,
       www.holocaustremembrance.com/resources/working-definition-
       antisemitism; "Letter to the Department of Education's Office for
       Civil Rights urging it not to use the IHRA definition of anti-Semitism
       and its examples to formulate antidiscrimination regulations,"
       Middle East Studies Association, June 27, 2022, www.mesana.org/
       advocacy/committee-on-academic-freedom/2022/06/27/letter-to-the-
       department-of-educations-office-for-civil-rights-urging-it-not-to-use-
       the-ihra-definition-of-anti-semitism-and-its-examples-to-formulate-
       antidiscrimination-regulations

112   The first generation of "New Historians" in the 1980s included Simha
       Flapan, *The Birth of Israel: Myths and Realities* (New York: Pantheon
       Books, 1987); Benny Morris, *The Birth of the Palestinian Refugee
       Problem, 1947–1949* (New York: Cambridge University Press, 1987); Ilan
       Pappe, *Britain and the Arab-Israeli Conflict, 1948–51* (Basingstoke:
       Palgrave Macmillan, 1988); Avi Shlaim, *Collusion across the Jordan:
       King Abdullah, the Zionist Movement, and the Partition of Palestine*

(New York: Columbia University Press, 1988). The discussion evolved
quickly to include Israeli sociologists and others, including Uri Ram,
Israeli Nationalism: Social Conflicts and the Politics of Knowledge
(Routledge, 2010); Rogan and Shlaim, *The War for Palestine*; Ariella
Azoulay, *From Palestine to Israel: A Photographic Record of Destruction
and State Formation, 1947–1950* (London: Pluto Press, 2011). Well
before this conversation began in Israel, the project of Zionism had been
critiqued by Arab, American, and European scholars from a variety
of fields. The discussion is far too broad to do justice to here, but see
Maxime Rodinson and Peter Buch, *Israel: A Colonial-Settler State?*,
trans. David Thorstad (New York: Pathfinder Press, 1973); Edward
W. Said, *The Question of Palestine* (New York: Times Books, 1979);
Rashid Khalidi, *Palestinian Identity: The Construction of Modern
National Consciousness* (New York: Columbia University Press, 1997).
More recent scholarship generally focuses on settler colonialism as a
paradigm: see Patrick Wolfe, "Settler Colonialism and the Elimination
of the Native," *Journal of Genocide Research* 8, no. 4 (2006): 387–409;
Alyosha Goldstein and Alex Lubin, eds., *Settler Colonialism, The South
Atlantic Quarterly* 107, no. 4 (Fall 2008) (Durham: Duke University
Press, 2008); Lorenzo Veracini, "The Other Shift: Settler Colonialism,
Israel, and the Occupation," *Journal of Palestine Studies* 42, no. 2 (2013):
26–42.

113   Emma Green, "Why the Charlottesville Marchers Were Obsessed With
       Jews," *The Atlantic* (blog), August 15, 2017, www.theatlantic.com/
       politics/archive/2017/08/nazis-racism-charlottesville/536928/

114   Danica Kirka, "London Pro-Palestinian March Passes off Peacefully but
       Police Clash with Far-Right Protesters," *AP News*, November 11, 2023,
       www.apnews.com/article/britain-israel-palestinian-protest-cenotaph-
       e57e2ec31af2fab16660161e5ed85ae8

115   "More than 20,000 People Join pro-Palestinian Rally in Brussels,"
       Reuters, November 11, 2023, www.reuters.com/world/more-than-
       20000-people-join-pro-palestinian-rally-brussels-2023-11-11/; "Photos:
       From Paris to Karachi, Protesters Rally in Support of Palestine," *Al
       Jazeera*, November 11, 2023, www.aljazeera.com/gallery/2023/11/11/
       photos-from-paris-to-karachi-protesters-rally-in-support-of-palestine

116   Aya Elamroussi and Rob Frehse, "Pro-Palestinian Protesters Snarl
       Manhattan Traffic and Limit Grand Central Access as They Call for
       Ceasefire Friday," *CNN*, November 11, 2023, www.cnn.com/2023/11/11/
       us/pro-palestine-protesters-new-york-city/index.html

117   Paul Messad, "Paris Sees Pro-Palestine, against Anti-Semitic Marches
       over Weekend, Macron Absent," *Euractiv*, November 13, 2023, www.
       euractiv.com/section/politics/news/paris-sees-pro-palestine-against-
       anti-semitic-marches-over-weekend-macron-absent/; Clea Caulcutt,
       "How a March against Antisemitism Became a Headache for Macron,"
       Politico, November 11, 2023, www.politico.eu/article/how-a-march-
       against-antisemitism-became-a-headache-for-macron/

118 "Hamas in 2017: The Document in Full," *Midde East Eye*, May 2, 2017, www.middleeasteye.net/news/hamas-2017-document-full

119 Tareq Baconi, *Hamas Contained: The Rise and Pacification of Palestinian Resistance* (Stanford: Stanford University Press, 2018), 104.

120 Elliott Colla, "On the History, Meaning, and Power of 'From the River To the Sea,'" *Mondoweiss*, November 16, 2023, www.mondoweiss.net/2023/11/on-the-history-meaning-and-power-of-from-the-river-to-the-sea/

121 Rashid Khalidi, "It's Time to Confront Israel's Version of 'From the River to the Sea,'" *The Nation*, November 22, 2023, www.thenation.com/article/world/its-time-to-confront-israels-version-of-from-the-river-to-the-sea/

122 Michael Barnett et al., "Israel's One-State Reality: It's Time to Give Up on the Two-State Solution," *Foreign Affairs*, April 14, 2023, www.foreignaffairs.com/middle-east/israel-palestine-one-state-solution

123 Michael Crowley and Edward Wong, "State Department Employees Send Blinken 'Dissent' Cables over Gaza Policy," *The New York Times*, November 13, 2023, www.nytimes.com/2023/11/13/us/politics/state-dept-israel-gaza-cease-fire.html

124 William D. Hartung, "Israel's War in Gaza, Subsidized by the USA," *The Nation*, November 10, 2023, www.thenation.com/article/politics/us-aid-israel-gaza/

125 "Update: Israel-Hamas War," *CNN*, November 13, 2023, www.cnn.com/middleeast/live-news/israel-hamas-war-gaza-news-11-13-23/index.html

126 Hind Khoudary, "A Month," Instagram, November 7, 2023, www.instagram.com/reel/CzXABUKrrYk/

127 Henry Carnell and Sam Van Pykeren, "He Claimed God Sent Hitler to Create Israel. Now He's Speaking at the Pro-Israel Rally. What?," *Mother Jones*, November 14, 2023, www.motherjones.com/politics/2023/11/john-hagee-hitler-israel-rally-christian-zionist/

128 Among many histories of evangelicals and prophecy, see Paul Boyer, *When Time Shall Be No More: Prophecy Belief in Modern American Culture* (Cambridge, MA: Belknap Press, 1993); Matthew Avery Sutton, *American Apocalypse: A History of Modern Evangelicalism* (Cambridge, MA: Belknap Press, 2014); Melani McAlister, *Epic Encounters: Culture, Media, and U.S. Interests in the Middle East Since 1945* (Berkeley: University of California Press, 2005), 155–97.

129 Tim LaHaye and Jerry B. Jenkins, *Left Behind: A Novel of the Earth's Last Days (Book 1)* (Wheaton: Tyndale House Publishers, Inc., 1995).

130 Hillary Kaell, *Walking Where Jesus Walked: American Christians and Holy Land Pilgrimage* (New York: NYU Press, 2014); Glenn Bowman, "The Politics of Tour Guiding: Israeli and Palestinian Guides," in *Tourism and the Less Developed Countries* (London: Belhaven Press, 1992).

131   Melani McAlister, "Prophecy, Politics, and the Popular: The Left Behind Series and Christian Fundamentalism's New World Order," *The South Atlantic Quarterly* 102, no. 4 (September 11, 2003): 773–98.

132   Walter Benjamin, "On the Concept of History," in *Illuminations* (New York: Schocken Books, 1986), 253–64.

133   Scott, *Conscripts of Modernity*, 44.

134   David Zimmermann, "Pro-Palestinian Protesters Stage Sit-In at *New York Times* Building, Accuse Media of Pro-Israel Bias," *National Review* (blog), November 10, 2023, www.nationalreview.com/news/pro-palestinian-protesters-stage-sit-in-at-new-york-times-building-accuse-media-of-pro-israel-bias/

135   Charlotte Klein, "'There Has Never Been Less Tolerance for This': Inside a *New York Times Magazine* Writer's Exit Over Gaza Letter," *Vanity Fair*, November 15, 2023, www.vanityfair.com/news/2023/11/new-york-times-gaza-letter-resignation; Katie Robertson, "*New York Times* Writer Resigns After Signing Letter Protesting the Israel-Gaza War," *The New York Times*, November 3, 2023, www.nytimes.com/2023/11/03/business/media/new-york-times-writer-resign-israel-gaza-war.html

136   William Sommer, "After Pulitzer Win, N.Y. Times Contributor Criticizes Gaza Coverage," *The Washington Post*, November 17, 2023, www.washingtonpost.com/style/media/2023/11/17/mona-chalabi-gaza-criticize-new-york-times-pulitzer/. In February 2024, *The Guardian* reports widespread disappointment and anger among CNN staff, who say that the tone of their coverage has been set from the top by their new Editor in Chief, Mark Thompson, who took the post two days after the Hamas attack. The staffers say that the assignments and reporting were skewed heavily toward Israel, and that guidance included tight restrictions on quoting Hamas or reporting Palestinian perspectives. Some said that every story on the conflict had to be cleared with the Jerusalem bureau before publication or broadcast. Chris McGreal, "CNN Staff Say Network's Pro-Israel Slant Amounts to 'Journalistic Malpractice,'" *The Guardian*, February 2, 2024, www.theguardian.com/media/2024/feb/04/cnn-staff-pro-israel-bias

137   Bethan McKernan, "Gaza's Main Hospital Has Become a 'Death Zone', Says WHO," *The Guardian*, November 19, 2023, www.theguardian.com/world/2023/nov/19/gazas-main-hospital-has-become-a-death-zone-says-who. On the legal issues regarding bombing hospitals, see Amanda Taub, "How International Law Views Military Action at a Hospital," *The New York Times*, November 16, 2023, www.nytimes.com/2023/11/16/world/middleeast/israel-hamas-al-shifa-hospital-law.html

138   Mosab Abu Toha, *Things You May Find Hidden in My Ear: Poems from Gaza* (San Francisco: City Lights Publishers, 2022).

139   Mosab Abu Toha, "The View from My Window in Gaza," *The New Yorker*, October 20, 2023, www.newyorker.com/news/the-weekend-essay/the-view-from-my-window-in-gaza

140   Raja Abdulrahim, "Noted Palestinian Poet Released by Israel After Two-Day Detention," *The New York Times*, November 21, 2023, www.nytimes.com/2023/11/21/world/middleeast/abu-toha-palestinian-poet-gaza.html; Chad De Guzman and Solcyré Burga, "Gaza-Based Poet Mosab Abu Toha Reunites With Family After Israeli Detention," *TIME*, November 21, 2023, www.time.com/6338183/palestinian-poet-mosab-abu-toha-arrested-gaza-israel/

141   Mosab Abu Toha, "A Harrowing Detention in Gaza," interview by David Remnick, *The New Yorker*, December 15, 2023, www.newyorker.com/podcast/the-new-yorker-radio-hour/a-harrowing-detention-in-gaza; Julian Borger, "Palestinian Poet Mosab Abu Toha Detained by Israelis in Gaza, Family Says," *The Guardian*, November 20, 2023, www.theguardian.com/world/2023/nov/20/palestinian-poet-mosab-abu-toha-arrested-by-israelis-in-gaza-family-says

142   Yousef Masoud and Daniel Victor, "More Than 100 Bodies Are Delivered to a Mass Grave in Southern Gaza," *The New York Times*, November 23, 2023, www.nytimes.com/2023/11/23/world/middleeast/gaza-mass-grave.html; "More than 100 People Buried in Mass Grave in Khan Younis," *Al Jazeera*, November 22, 2023, www.aljazeera.com/program/newsfeed/2023/11/22/more-than-100-people-buried-in-mass-grave-in-khan-younis

143   McAlister, *Epic Encounters*, 198–234.

144   Aslı Ü. Bâli and Laurie Brand, "Letter to the University of Pennsylvania Protesting Its Decision to Ban the Screening of the Documentary Israelism," Middle East Studies Association, December 1, 2023, www.mesana.org/advocacy/committee-on-academic-freedom/2023/12/01/letter-to-the-university-of-pennsylvania-protesting-its-decision-to-ban-the-screening-of-the-documentary-israelism

145   "Committee on Academic Freedom," Middle East Studies Association, November 21, 2023, www.mesana.org/advocacy/committee-on-academic-freedom

146   Joshua Hammer, "The Death of Rachel Corrie," *Mother Jones*, October 2003, www.motherjones.com/politics/2003/09/death-rachel-corrie/

147   Sara Ahmed, *The Cultural Politics of Emotion* (New York: Routledge, 2004), 10.

148   Sara Ahmed, *The Promise of Happiness* (Durham: Duke University Press, 2010), 199.

149   Alex Lubin, *Geographies of Liberation: The Making of an Afro-Arab Political Imaginary* (Chapel Hill: The University of NC Press, 2014); Piero Gleijeses, *Conflicting Missions: Havana, Washington, and Africa, 1959–1976* (Chapel Hill: The University of NC Press, 2003); Judy Tzu-Chun Wu, *Radicals on the Road: Internationalism, Orientalism, and Feminism during the Vietnam Era* (Ithaca: Cornell University Press, 2013).

150 Vijay Prashad, *The Darker Nations: A People's History of the Third World* (New York: The New Press, 2008).

151 Robert Vitalis, "The Midnight Ride of Kwame Nkrumah and Other Fables of Bandung (Ban-Doong)," *Humanity* 4, no. 2 (2013): 261–88; Christopher J. Lee, ed., *Making a World after Empire: The Bandung Moment and Its Political Afterlives* (Athens: Ohio University Press, 2010).

152 Atalia Omer and Joshua Lupo, "Introduction," in *Religion and Broken Solidarities: Feminism, Race, and Transnationalism* (Notre Dame, Indiana: University of Notre Dame Press, 2022), 5.

153 Elly Bulkin, Minnie Bruce Pratt, and Barbara Smith, *Yours in Struggle: Three Feminist Perspectives on Anti-Semitism and Racism* (Ithaca: Firebrand Books, 1984).

154 Bill Hutchinson, "Palestinian-American Student Issues Message after He and 2 Friends Shot in Vermont," *ABC News*, November 28, 2023, www.abcnews.go.com/US/palestinian-student-wounded-vermont-shooting-breaks-silence-message/story?id=105220579; Juliana Kim, "Palestinian Student Shot in Vermont Is Paralyzed from Chest Down, His Family Says," *NPR*, December 3, 2023, www.npr. org/2023/12/03/1216852611/palestinian-student-shot-in-vermont-is-paralyzed-from-chest-down-his-family-says

155 Suhaib Salem and Nidal Al-Mughrabi, "Scores Reported Killed in Gaza as Fighting Shatters Israel-Hamas Truce," *Reuters*, December 1, 2023, www.reuters.com/world/middle-east/gaza-negotiators-try-get-israel-hamas-agree-extend-truce-again-2023-12-01/

156 "Israel orders Gazans to flee, bombs where it sends them," *Reuters*, December 4, 2023, www.reuters.com/video/watch/ idRW320104122023RP1/

157 Katherine Knott, "3 Presidents on the Hot Seat," *Inside Higher Ed*, December 5, 2023, www.insidehighered.com/news/government/2023/ 12/05/house-republicans-castigate-presidents-harvard-penn-and-mit

158 Ellen Schrecker, "Political Repression and the *AAUP* from 1915 to the Present," *AAUP*, October 10, 2023, www.aaup.org/article/political-repression-and-aaup-1915-present; Nancy MacLean, *Democracy in Chains: The Deep History of the Radical Right's Stealth Plan for America* (New York: Penguin Random House, 2017).

159 Ultimately, McGill and Gay would each lose their jobs largely because of the fallout from this hearing.

160 Sana Noor Haq and Abeer Salman, "Prominent Gaza Professor and Writer Killed in Airstrike, Weeks after Telling *CNN* He and His Family Had 'Nowhere Else to Go,'" *CNN*, December 11, 2023, www.cnn. com/2023/12/11/middleeast/refaat-alareer-gaza-professor-killed-in-airstrike-intl/index.html

161   Refaat Alareer, ed., *Gaza Writes Back: Short Stories from Young Writers in Gaza, Palestine* (Charlottesville: Just World Books, 2014); Refaat Alareer and Laila M. El-Haddad, eds., *Gaza Unsilenced* (Charlottesville: Just World Books, 2015).

162   *Stories Make Us | Refaat Alareer | TEDxShujaiya* (Shujaiya, 2015), www.youtube.com/watch?v=YsbEjldJjOw

163   Refaat Alareer, "My Child Asks, 'Can Israel Destroy Our Building If the Power Is Out?'," *The New York Times*, May 13, 2021, www.nytimes.com/2021/05/13/opinion/israel-gaza-rockets-airstrikes.html

164   Refaat Alareer, "Refaat in Gaza," X (Twitter), November 1, 2023, www.x.com/itranslate123

165   Noor Hindi, "Fuck Your Lecture on Craft, My People Are Dying," *Poetry Magazine*, December 2020, www.poetryfoundation.org/poetrymagazine/poems/154658/fuck-your-lecture-on-craft-my-people-are-dying

166   Augusta Saraiva, "UN Steps Up Gaza Cease-Fire Calls With Strongest Move Since 1971," *Bloomberg*, December 6, 2023, www.bloomberg.com/news/articles/2023-12-06/un-chief-steps-up-pressure-for-gaza-cease-fire-with-rare-appeal; "Secretary-General Urges Security Council to Call for Ceasefire in Gaza, Declaring That Humanitarian Situation Is Now at 'Breaking Point'" (United Nations: Meetings Coverage and Press Releases, December 6, 2023), press.un.org/en/2023/sc15518.doc.htm

167   Eileen S. Kuttab, "Palestinian Women in the 'Intifada': Fighting on Two Fronts," *Arab Studies Quarterly* 15, no. 2 (1993): 69–85; Graham Usher, "Palestinian Women, the Intifada and the State of Independence: An Interview with Rita Giacaman," *Race & Class* 34, no. 3 (1993): 31–43.

168   Joel Brinkley, "Inside the Intifada," *The New York Times*, October 29, 1989, www.nytimes.com/1989/10/29/magazine/inside-the-intifada.html

169   Zachary Lockman and Joel Beinin, *Intifada: The Palestinian Uprising against Israeli Occupation* (Boston: South End Press, 1989).

170   Robert Brym and Bader Araj, "Suicide Bombing as Strategy and Interaction: The Case of the Second Intifada," *Social Forces* 84, no. 4 (June 2006): 1970.

171   "What Does 'Globalize the Intifada' Mean and How Can It Lead to Targeting Jews with Violence?," American Jewish Committee, December 4, 2023, www.ajc.org/news/what-does-globalize-the-intifada-mean-and-how-can-it-lead-to-targeting-jews-with-violence; Robert Tait, "What's Behind the Antisemitism Furor over College Presidents' Testimony?," *The Guardian*, December 12, 2023, www.theguardian.com/us-news/2023/dec/12/university-president-antisemitism-israel-palestine-explained-harvard-penn

172   *"I Am You": NYC Vigil Honors Palestinian Poet Dr. Refaat Alareer* (New York, 2023), www.youtube.com/watch?v=nZE7YnRIXtg

173 The BDS Movement page lays out the parameters of institutional boycotts here: www.bdsmovement.net/academic-boycott. In the early days of the boycott, however, some people interpreted the boycott more individually: Israeli academics were removed from editorial boards, collaborations with Israeli scholars were sometimes halted.

174 Michael Roth, "Boycott of Israeli Universities: A Repugnant Attack on Academic Freedom," *Los Angeles Times*, December 19, 2013, www.latimes.com/opinion/la-xpm-2013-dec-19-la-oe-roth-academic-boycott-israel-20131219-story.html; Leon Wieseltier, "The Academic Boycott of Israel Is a Travesty," *The New Republic*, December 17, 2013, www.newrepublic.com/article/115961/american-studies-association-boycott-israel-travesty

175 Peter Schmidt, "Backlash Against Israel Boycott Throws Academic Association on Defensive," *The New York Times*, January 5, 2014, www.nytimes.com/2014/01/06/us/backlash-against-israel-boycott-throws-academic-association-on-defensive.html

176 Mahmoud Darwish, *Memory for Forgetfulness: August, Beirut, 1982*, trans. Ibrahim Muhawi, with a new foreword by Sinan Antoon (Berkeley: University of California Press, 2013). A very useful critical analysis of the book is in Tahia Abdel Nasser, *Literary Autobiography and Arab National Struggles* (Edinburgh: Edinburgh University Press, 2017).

177 Darwish, *Memory for Forgetfulness*, 22.

178 Darwish, *Memory for Forgetfulness*, 49.

179 Darwish, *Memory for Forgetfulness*, 11.

180 Darwish, *Memory for Forgetfulness*, 180.

181 Ishaan Tharoor, "The Israeli Right Hopes Not Just for Victory in Gaza, but Also Conquest," *The Washington Post*, November 19, 2023, www.washingtonpost.com/world/2023/11/17/israel-government-right-gaza-endgame-conquest/

182 Tony Karon and Daniel Levy, "Israel Is Losing This War," *The Nation*, December 8, 2023, www.thenation.com/article/world/israel-gaza-war/

183 David Gilmour, "'How Can There Be Peace?': Anchor Stunned As Israeli Ambassador 'Absolutely' Rejects Two-State Solution," *Media-ite*, December 14, 2023, www.mediaite.com/uk/anchor-stunned-as-israeli-ambassador-hotovely-absolutely-rejects-two-state-solution/

184 Alice Austin, "Families of Israeli Hostages Cling to Waning Hope," *+972 Magazine*, December 13, 2023, www.972mag.com/israeli-hostages-gaza-families-hope/; Nancy A. Youssef et al., "Israel Begins Pumping Seawater Into Hamas's Gaza Tunnels," *WSJ*, December 13, 2023, www.wsj.com/world/middle-east/israel-hamas-war-pumping-seawater-gaza-tunnels-2ed3b3f2

185 Josh Breiner, "Israeli Security Establishment: Hamas Likely Didn't Have Advance Knowledge of Nova Festival," *Haaretz*, November 18, 2023,

www.haaretz.com/israel-news/2023-11-18/ty-article/.premium/israeli-security-establishment-hamas-likely-didnt-have-prior-knowledge-of-nova-festival/0000018b-e2ee-d168-a3ef-f7fe8ca20000; Noa Limone, "If Israel Used a Controversial Procedure against Its Citizens, We Need to Talk about It Now," *Haaretz*, December 13, 2023, www.haaretz.com/opinion/2023-12-13/ty-article-opinion/.premium/if-israel-used-a-procedure-against-its-citizens-we-need-to-talk-about-it-now/0000018c-6383-de43-affd-f783212e0000

186   They're not alone: both *The New York Times* and *The Washington Post* were, especially in the first month or so of the war, distinctly more invested in telling Israeli stories than Palestinian ones. *The Intercept* would later produce a study of more than 1,000 articles from *The New York Times*, *The Washington Post*, and *The Los Angeles Times*. Their comparison showed that, during the first six weeks of the war, Israeli deaths were covered disproportionately to their numbers, and that words like "slaughter," "massacre," and "horrific" were reserved almost exclusively for Israeli deaths. The term "slaughter," for example, was used to describe the killing of Israelis versus Palestinians at a rate of 60:1. Adam Johnson and Othman Ali, "Coverage of Gaza War in *The New York Times* and Other Major Newspapers," *The Intercept*, January 9, 2024, www.theintercept.com/2024/01/09/newspapers-israel-palestine-bias-new-york-times

187   "Watch Clarissa Ward Report From Inside Gaza for the First Time Since War Began," *CNN*, December 14, 2023, www.cnn.com/videos/world/2023/12/14/gaza-on-the-ground-clarissa-ward-pkg-intl-ldn-vpx.cnn

188   Faculty for Justice in Palestine-Syracuse University chapter, "Statement of Solidarity in Opposition to the Repressive Climate on College Campuses," www.linktr.ee/fjp_su; see also Gemma Ware, "Israel-Gaza War is Having a Chilling Effect on Academic Freedom – Podcast," *The Conversation*, December 18, 2023, www.theconversation.com/israel-gaza-war-is-having-a-chilling-effect-on-academic-freedom-podcast-219926. For an important discussion on academic freedom debates in the Israeli-Palestine context, see Judith Butler, "Israel/Palestine and the Paradoxes of Academic Freedom," *Radical Philosophy*, no. 135 (2006): 8–17.

189   Ruwaida Kamal Amer, "Gaza's Rescue Workers Are Haunted by Those They Couldn't Save," *+972 Magazine*, December 19, 2023, www.972mag.com/gaza-civil-defense-rescue-workers-rubble/

190   Joelle M. Abi-Rached, "The War on Hospitals," *Boston Review*, December 20, 2023, www.bostonreview.net/articles/the-war-on-hospitals/

191   Ezra Klein, "Ezra Klein on Gaza, A.I. and the 2024 Elections," *The Ezra Klein Show*, accessed June 29, 2024, www.nytimes.com/2023/12/20/podcasts/transcript-ezra-klein-ask-me-anything.html

192   "Israel: Discriminatory Land Policies Hem in Palestinians," Human Rights Watch, May 12, 2020, www.hrw.org/news/2020/05/12/israel-discriminatory-land-policies-hem-palestinians

193   Matthew Frye Jacobson, *Whiteness of a Different Color: European Immigrants and the Alchemy of Race* (Cambridge, MA: Harvard University Press, 1999); Thomas A Guglielmo, *White on Arrival: Italians, Race, Color, and Power in Chicago, 1890–1945* (New York: Oxford University Press, 2003).

194   Abby Budiman, Christine Tamir, Lauren Mora and Luis Noe-Bustamante, "Facts on U.S. Immigrants, 2018," *Pew Research Center's Hispanic Trends Project* (blog), August 20, 2020, www.pewresearch.org/hispanic/2020/08/20/facts-on-u-s-immigrants/

195   A. Naomi Paik, *Bans, Walls, Raids, Sanctuary: Understanding U.S. Immigration for the Twenty-First Century* (Berkeley: University of California Press, 2020).

196   Bradley R. Simpson, "Self-Determination, Human Rights, and the End of Empire in the 1970s," *Humanity Journal* 4, no. 2 (Summer 2013): 239–60.

197   "Israel's War on the Palestinians w/ Amjad Iraqi," *Politics Theory Other* (podcast), accessed June 4, 2024, www.patreon.com/poltheoryother; "Transcript: Ezra Klein Interviews Amjad Iraqi," *The New York Times*, November 7, 2023, www.nytimes.com/2023/11/07/podcasts/ezra-klein-interviews-amjad-iraqi.html

198   Malka Older, *Infomocracy: Book One of the Centenal Cycle* (New York: Tor.com, 2017).

199   Mark Landler, "Five Miles and a World Apart, Younger Activists Dream of a New Peace Process," *The New York Times*, November 16, 2023, www.nytimes.com/2023/11/16/world/middleeast/israel-palestinians-new-peace-plans.html

200   Liza Rozovsky, Josh Breiner, and Ido Efrati, "Sexual Violence Evidence against Hamas Is Mounting, but the Road to Court Is Still Long," *Haaretz*, November 22, 2023, www.haaretz.com/israel-news/2023-11-22/ty-article-magazine/.premium/sexual-assault-evidence-against-hamas-is-mounting-but-the-road-to-court-is-still-long/0000018b-f6bb-dafe-a18f-f7fb0a570000; Physicians for Social Responsibility, "Sexual and Gender-Based Violence as a Weapon of War During the October 7, 2023 Hamas Attacks" (Tel Aviv, November 2023).

201   Jonathan Cook, "Hamas 'Mass Rape' Claim Lacks Evidence. But It's Being Used to Justify Genocide," Substack newsletter, *Jonathan Cook* (blog), December 18, 2023, jonathancook.substack.com/p/hamas-mass-rape-claim-lacks-evidence

202   Samah Salaime, "Women's Liberation Mustn't Stop at Either Side of the Gaza Fence," *+972 Magazine*, December 22, 2023, www.972mag.com/palestinian-jewish-feminists-women-liberation-gaza-fence/

203   Nidal Al-Mughrabi, "Israeli Images Showing Palestinian Detainees in Underwear Spark Outrage," *Reuters*, December 8, 2023, www.reuters.com/world/middle-east/hamas-condemns-israel-over-images-showing-semi-naked-palestinian-prisoners-2023-12-08/

204   China Miéville, *The City & The City*, (New York: Del Rey, 2010).

205   Donna J. Haraway, *Staying with the Trouble: Making Kin in the Chthulucene* (Durham: Duke University Press Books, 2016), 1.

206   Khalil Shikaki, "Public Opinion Poll : Migration of Palestinian Christians," Palestinian Center for Policy and Survey Research, February 23, 2020, www.pcpsr.org/en/node/806

207   Justin Welby and Hosam Naoum, "Let Us Pray for the Christians Being Driven from the Holy Land," *The Times*, December 24, 2023, www.thetimes.co.uk/article/let-us-pray-for-the-christians-being-driven-from-the-holy-land-f27wwksdh

208   "Israel Travel & Tourism Statistics for 2023," Tourist Israel: The Guide, January 31, 2022, www.touristisrael.com/israel-travel-tourism-statistics/53929/; Maayan Jaffe-Hoffman, "2.5 Mil. Christians Visited Israel in 2019. Post-COVID, Will They Return?" *The Jerusalem Post*, October 22, 2021, www.jpost.com/health-and-wellness/coronavirus/will-covid-19-keep-christians-from-visiting-israel-again-682779. Israeli statistics count visitors to the West Bank as visitors to Israel.

209   Yara Bayoumy and Samar Hazboun, "'God Is Under the Rubble in Gaza': Bethlehem's Subdued Christmas," *The New York Times*, December 23, 2023, www.nytimes.com/2023/12/23/world/middleeast/israel-gaza-bethlehem-christmas.html

210   Evan Hill et al., "Israel Has Waged One of This Century's Most Destructive Wars in Gaza," *The Washington Post*, December 23, 2023, www.washingtonpost.com/investigations/interactive/2023/israel-war-destruction-gaza-record-pace/; Julia Frankel, "Israel's Military Campaign in Gaza is among the Most Destructive in History, Experts Say," *PBS NewsHour*, December 21, 2023, www.pbs.org/newshour/world/israels-military-campaign-in-gaza-is-among-the-most-destructive-in-history-experts-say

211   Omar Abdel-Baqui, "More U.N. Workers Killed in Israel-Gaza War Than in Any Single Conflict," *WSJ*, November 6, 2023, www.wsj.com/livecoverage/israel-hamas-war-gaza-strip-2023-11-06/card/more-u-n-workers-killed-in-israel-gaza-war-than-in-any-single-conflict-zmn8HI8KVoYHvQCQ3vac

212   "Gaza War 'Most Dangerous Ever' for Journalists, Says Rights Group," *Reuters*, December 21, 2023, www.reuters.com/world/middle-east/gaza-war-most-dangerous-ever-journalists-says-rights-group-2023-12-21/

213   www.west-eastern-divan.org/; www.standing-together.org/en; www.972mag.com

214   Haggai Ram, *Intoxicating Zion: A Social History of Hashish in Mandatory Palestine and Israel* (Stanford: Stanford University Press, 2020).

215   Devi Sridhar, "It's Not Just Bullets and Bombs. I Have Never Seen Health Organisations as Worried as They Are About Disease in Gaza," *The Guardian*, December 29, 2023, www.theguardian.com/commentisfree/2023/dec/29/health-organisations-disease-gaza-population-outbreaks-conflict

216   Ibtisam Mahdi, "Gaza's Health Crisis 'Catastrophic,' Say Palestinian Experts," *+972 Magazine*, December 20, 2023, www.972mag.com/gaza-health-crisis-disease/

217   Abigail Williams and Megan Lebowitz, "Biden Administration Sidesteps Congress Again for Emergency Arms Sale to Israel," *NBC News*, December 30, 2023, www.nbcnews.com/politics/white-house/biden-administration-sidesteps-congress-arms-sale-israel-rcna131661

218   John Hudson and Mikhail Klimentov, "U.S. Approves $147.5 Million Sale of Artillery Ammunition and Gear to Israel," *The Washington Post*, December 30, 2023, www.washingtonpost.com/national-security/2023/12/30/us-weapons-sale-israel-blinken/

219   See, for example, Mahmoud Darwish, *A River Dies of Thirst* (New York: Archipelago Books, 2009).

220   "Mahmoud Darwish's Welcome Letter to the Inaugural Palestine Festival of Literature," The Palestine Festival of Literature, May 8, 2008, www.palfest.org/mahmoud-darwish-welcome

221   Lara-Nour Walton, "Inside the Gaza Solidarity Encampment at Columbia University," *The Nation*, April 19, 2024, www.thenation.com/article/activism/columbia-university-gaza-solidarity-encampment-cuad-palestine-protest/

222   IER, "Renewable Energy Still Dominates Energy Subsidies in FY 2022," *IER* (blog), August 9, 2023, www.instituteforenergyresearch.org/fossil-fuels/renewable-energy-still-dominates-energy-subsidies-in-fy-2022/

223   Liam Stack et al., "Parts of Gaza in 'Full-Blown Famine,' U.N. Aid Official Says," *The New York Times*, May 4, 2024, www.nytimes.com/2024/05/04/world/middleeast/gaza-famine-mccain-israel.html

224   "More Children Killed in Gaza in Four Months than in Four Years of War Globally: Report," *MSNBC*, March 14, 2024, www.msnbc.com/top-stories/latest/death-toll-children-gaza-israel-rcna143269

225   Carmen Molina Acosta, "Over 75% of All Journalists Killed in 2023 Died in Gaza War, per CPJ," *ICIJ*, February 16, 2024, www.icij.org/inside-icij/2024/02/over-75-of-all-journalists-killed-in-2023-died-in-gaza-war-per-cpj/

FURTHER READING

HISTORICAL AND POLITICAL ANALYSIS

Allen, Lori. *A History of False Hope: Investigative Commissions in Palestine*. Stanford: Stanford University Press, 2020.

Anziska, Seth. *Preventing Palestine: A Political History from Camp David to Oslo*. Princeton: Princeton University Press, 2020.

Baconi, Tareq. *Hamas Contained: The Rise and Pacification of Palestinian Resistance*. Stanford: Stanford University Press, 2018.

Beinart, Peter. *The Crisis of Zionism*. New York: Times Books, 2012.

Benin, Joel, and Lisa Hajjar. "Palestine-Israel Primer." *MERIP*, April 2014. www.merip.org/palestine-israel-primer/

Bishara, Amahl. *Back Stories: U.S. News Production and Palestinian Politics*. Stanford: Stanford University Press, 2012.

Brown, Nathan. *Palestinian Politics after the Oslo Accords: Resuming Arab Palestine*. Berkeley: University of California Press, 2003.

Elgindy, Khaled. *Blind Spot: America and the Palestinians, from Balfour to Trump*. Washington, D.C: Brookings Institution Press, 2019.

Erakat, Noura. *Justice for Some: Law and the Question of Palestine.* Stanford: Stanford University Press, 2019.

Feldman, Ilana. *Life Lived in Relief: Humanitarian Predicaments and Palestinian Refugee Politics.* Oakland: University of California Press, 2018.

Gordon, Neve. *Israel's Occupation.* Berkeley: University of California Press, 2008.

Hahn, Peter L. *Crisis and Crossfire: The United States and the Middle East Since 1945.* Washington, D.C: Potomac Books, 2005.

Hajjar, Lisa. *Courting Conflict: The Israeli Military Court System in the West Bank and Gaza.* Berkeley: University of California Press, 2005.

Hill, Marc Lamont, and Mitchell Plitnick. *Except for Palestine: The Limits of Progressive Politics.* New York: The New Press, 2022.

Kaplan, Amy. *Our American Israel: The Story of an Entangled Alliance.* Cambridge, MA: Harvard University Press, 2018.

Khalidi, Rashid. *The Hundred Years' War on Palestine: A History of Settler Colonialism and Resistance, 1917-2017.* New York, Metropolitan Books, 2020.

Levin, Geoffrey. *Our Palestine Question: Israel and American Jewish Dissent, 1948-1978.* New Haven: Yale University Press, 2023.

Loewenstein, Antony. *The Palestine Laboratory: How Israel Exports the Technology of Occupation Around the World.* New York: Verso, 2023.

Makdisi, Saree. *Tolerance Is a Wasteland: Palestine and the Culture of Denial.* Oakland: University of California Press, 2022.

Makdisi, Saree, and Alice Walker. *Palestine Inside Out: An Everyday Occupation.* New York: W. W. Norton & Company, 2010.

Makdisi, Ussama. *Faith Misplaced: The Broken Promise of U.S.-Arab Relations: 1820-2001.* New York: PublicAffairs, 2010.

Mitelpunkt, Shaul. *Israel in the American Mind: The Cultural Politics of US-Israeli Relations, 1958-1988.* Cambridge: Cambridge University Press, 2018.

Pennock, Pamela E. *The Rise of the Arab American Left: Activists, Allies, and Their Fight against Imperialism and Racism, 1960s–1980s.* Chapel Hill: The University of North Carolina Press, 2017.

Roy, Sara. *Unsilencing Gaza: Reflections on Resistance.* London: Pluto Press, 2021.

Roy, Sara. *Failing Peace: Gaza and the Palestinian-Israeli Conflict.* London: Pluto Press, 2007.

Sa'di, Ahmad H., and Lila Abu-Lughod, eds. *Nakba: Palestine, 1948, and the Claims of Memory.* New York: Columbia University Press, 2007.

Said, Edward W. *The Selected Works of Edward Said, 1966–2006.* Edited by Moustafa Bayoumi and Andrew Rubin. Expanded edition. New York: Vintage, 2019.

Schulman, Sarah. *Israel/Palestine and the Queer International.* Durham: Duke University Press, 2012.

Seikaly, Sherene. "The Matter of Time." *The American Historical Review* 124, no. 5 (2019): 1681–88.

Shehadeh, Raja. *What Does Israel Fear From Palestine?* New York: Other Press, 2024.

Telhami, Shibley, Marc Lynch, Nathan J. Brown, and Michael Barnett. *The One State Reality: What Is Israel/Palestine?* Ithaca: Cornell University Press, 2023.

Thrall, Nathan. *A Day in the Life of Abed Salama: Anatomy of a Jerusalem Tragedy.* New York: Metropolitan Books, 2023.

Weizman, Eyal. *Hollow Land: Israel's Architecture of Occupation.* London: Verso, 2024.

LITERATURE AND MEMOIR

Abu Toha, Mosab. *Things You May Find Hidden in My Ear: Poems from Gaza.* San Francisco: City Lights Publishers, 2022.

Abulhawa, Susan. *Against the Loveless World*. New York: Washington Square Press, 2021.

Abusalim, Jehad, Jennifer Bing, and Mike Merryman-Lotze, eds. *Light in Gaza: Writings Born of Fire*. Chicago: Haymarket Books, 2022.

Alareer, Refaat, ed. *Gaza Writes Back: Short Stories from Young Writers in Gaza, Palestine*. Charlottesville: Just World Books, 2014.

Alyan, Hala. *Salt Houses*. Boston: Houghton Mifflin Harcourt, 2017.

Azoulay, Ariella. *From Palestine to Israel: A Photographic Record of Destruction and State Formation, 1947–1950*. London: Pluto Press, 2011.

Barghouti, Mourid. *I Saw Ramallah*. Translated by Ahdaf Soueif. New York: Anchor, 2003.

Darwish, Mahmoud. *Unfortunately, It Was Paradise: Selected Poems*. Edited by Sinan Antoon and Amira El-Zein. Translated by Munir Akash and Carolyn Forché. Berkeley: University of California Press, 2013.

Habiby, Emile. *The Secret Life of Saeed: The Pessoptimist*. Translated by Salma Khadra Jayyusi. Brooklyn: Interlink Pub Group, 2001.

Hindi, Noor. *Dear God. Dear Bones. Dear Yellow*. Chicago: Haymarket Books, 2022.

Kanafani, Ghassan. *Men in the Sun and Other Palestinian Stories*. Washington, D.C.: Three Continents Press, 1978.

Khalifeh, Sahar. *Passage to the Plaza*. Translated by Sawad Hussain. London: Seagull Books, 2020.

Khoury, Elias. *Gate of the Sun*. Translated by Humphrey Davies. New York: Archipelago Books, 2016.

Nye, Naomi Shihab. *The Tiny Journalist*. Rochester: BOA Editions, 2019.

Soueif, Ahdaf, and Omar Robert Hamilton eds. *This Is Not a Border: Reportage & Reflection from the Palestine Festival of Literature*. New York: Bloomsbury, 2017.

WEB RESOURCES AND MAGAZINES

Jadaliyya at www.jadaliyya.com. News and analysis about the Middle
East broadly but has a particularly strong series on Gaza
and another on attacks on academic freedom in the US.

Jewish Currents at www.jewishcurrents.org. Award-winning magazine
of the US Jewish Left, with critical reporting on Israel
and Palestine.

Middle East Report at www.merip.org. Scholarly and timely articles on
a wide range of Middle East issues.

Visualizing Palestine at www.visualizingpalestine.org. Wonderful, clear
graphics and posters for use in education or activism. Free to download
and use.

+972 Magazine at www.972mag.com. Independent journalism from
Israel and Palestine by a variety of contributors on the ground.
Indispensable.

ACKNOWLEDGMENTS

The following organizations will receive the author's royalties from this book: Anera, a relief and development organization (Washington, DC); the Committee to Protect Journalists (New York); Jewish Voice for Peace (New York); PalFest: the Palestinian Festival of Literature (Ramallah); and Visualizing Palestine (Toronto).

My debts for the writing of this book are many. I was deeply grateful that friends and allies of all sorts jumped in to help me think about this project on its winding path to becoming the book it finally did. I owe a special thanks to my friend and Radcliffe colleague Joelle Abi-Rached, who insisted early on that the scattered journal entries I shared with her should become a book. I am also very thankful to Jess Gough at MACK for her belief in the book and her hard work on making it better. The press overall has been wonderful to work with, and I am grateful to Laleh Khalili for suggesting I reach out to them. Thanks also to Louis Rogers at MACK for his marvelous copyediting, and to Bedirhan Mutlu, who fact-checked the final manuscript and saved me from a humbling number of mistakes. Whatever errors remain are my own. A special thank you to Dia al-Azzawi for permission to use part of his masterwork, *Sabra and Shatila Massacre* (1982–83), in the cover design. Thanks also to Kate Brown and Mark Bradley at the *American Historical Review*, who were generous and enthusiastic in publishing a piece of this essay in *AHR* volume 129, issue 3 (September 2023).

Many other people have read and commented on drafts of shorter or longer versions. Thank you to Meagan Black, Sneeha Bose, Jimena Canales, Elliott Colla, Ruth Feldstein, Ted German, Tom Guglielmo, David Hollinger, Dina Khoury, Laleh Lalami, Robert G. Lee, Alex Lubin, Carla Lillvik, Justin Mann, Ann Munson, Tony Palomba, Uta Poiger, Doug Rossinow, Gayle Wald, and Nancy Wechsler. I am especially grateful to Sarah Gualtieri, Zachary Lockman, and Zaynab Quadri, who read closely and at key moments. Thanks also to the history department at Northeastern University for inviting me to present part of this work in progress. To all of you: your insights and generosity have meant the world to me.

I started writing this book on a Harvard Radcliffe Fellowship, and I received wonderful support from the staff there, including Executive Director Claudia Rizzini and Associate Director Sharon Bromberg-Lim. I also had, over the course of the year, four excellent undergraduate research assistants. Thank you to Ismail Assafi, Austin Grant, Mia Lupicia, and Charlotte Ritz-Jack. I also owe great debt to those who wrote letters of recommendation for this (and many other) applications: Mark Bradley, Marwan Kraidy, Penny Von Eschen, and Salim Yaqub.

This book was inspired by the political energy and unswerving commitment to justice amongst many of my Radcliffe cohort: thank you so much to those who debated, texted, marched, supported, and consoled during our time together.

My year in Cambridge was made possible by the support of GWU'S Columbian College, as well as a grant from the American Philosophical Society. I am also grateful to my colleagues in GW's department of American Studies and the Institute for Middle East Studies for being such wonderful interlocutors and allies. Other supporters of the Cambridge year included my beloved friends there: Carla Lillvik, Ann Munson, and Uta Poiger, as well as Megan Black, Wan Chi Lau, Nancy Wechsler, and Ella Wechsler-Matthei.

My longest and deepest intellectual debts are also intertwined with friendship, political discussions, and much wine. Thank you to my DC-area reading group of many years, whose current members include Libby Anker, Mona Atia, Elliott Colla, Ilana Feldman, Despina Kakoudaki, Dina Khoury, and Aman Luthra. In addition, I am grateful for the friendships of Gayle Wald, Kelly Pemberton, Ruth Feldstein, David Brown, Wendy Eudy, and Julie McAlister.

As Israel's war on Gaza unfolded, I deeply missed the wisdom and friendship of Amy Kaplan (1955–2020). Her work has been an inspiration to so many of us who study the US relations with Israel and/or the politics of culture. She was a dear friend for more than two decades, and I have felt the loss of her voice keenly over the last year.

First, last, and always, I owe my partner Carl more gratitude than I can say. From putting up with my departure from home for much of the academic year to taking care of our house and our three spoiled cats while I enjoyed the delights of a fellowship, he has been material support that made this work possible. But, far more than that, he is my intellectual and political companion: our conversations, my reading of his work, his comments on my writing—all of it is a gift that still leaves me in awe. Our life together is everything; it's the wonder that's keeping the stars apart.

ALSO FROM THIS SERIES

DISCOURSE is a series of small books in which a theorist, artist, or writer engages in a dialogue with a theme, an artwork, an idea, or another individual across an extended text.

Melani McAlister
Promises, Then the Storm: Notes on Memory, Protest, and the Israel-Gaza War

First edition published by MACK
© 2024 MACK for this edition
© 2024 Melani McAlister for her text

Designed by Tilly Sleven
Edited by Jess Gough
Copyedited by Louis Rogers
Printed by KOPA

ISBN 978-1-915743-62-6
mackbooks.us